BY THE WAY...

Praise for Algy Cluff's
previous books

Get On With It

'At seventy-six, he reflects in this memoir on a blissful sounding life at home and abroad – high jinks in the Army, languorous City luncheons primed by pink gins, drilling successfully for oil in the North Sea, mining diamonds in Africa and becoming friendly with such disparate figures as Margaret Thatcher and Zimbabwe's notorious President Robert Mugabe…

'Enjoyably gossipy, *Get On With It* also contains valuable insights into business and political life… Appropriately, playwright Sir Tom Stoppard suggests his next book should be called *The Importance Of Being Algy.*'
—*Daily Mail*

'… one of the few books I'd read which I wished longer…'
—Charles Moore, *The Spectator*

'When he was a small boy at boarding school in the 1940s, Algy Cluff's imagination was captivated by hectic tales of derring-do in the novels of John Buchan. He resolved then to actualise this imaginary world of clubland heroes. For the past half-century he has been, as this rattling, full-throttled, red-blooded memoir shows, a strenuous, venturesome capitalist in Richard Hannay's mould.'

—Richard Davenport-Hines, *TLS*

'A cross-pollination of James Bond and Indiana Jones, with an eye for adventure and a real talent for entrepreneurship.'

—*KCW Today*

***

Unsung Heroes

'… a splendid book…'

—*The Times*

'I warmly recommend it… Although Algy's own life has been extremely active and successful, his greatest gift is for describing, affectionately, lives of which this could not be said.'

—Charles Moore, *The Spectator*

By the Way…

Algy Cluff

Cluff & Sons

First published in Great Britain in 2019 by Cluff & Sons

Copyright © J. G. Cluff 2019

J. G. Cluff has asserted his right under the Copyright, Designs and Patents Act 1988 to be identified as the author of this work.

Edited, designed and produced by Tandem Publishing
http://tandempublishing.yolasite.com/

ISBN: 978-1-52723-543-4

10 9 8 7 6 5 4 3 2 1

A CIP catalogue record for this book is available from the British Library.

Printed and bound in Great Britain by CPI Group (UK) Ltd, Croydon CR0 4YY.

To Henry and Tessa Keswick

Also by Algy Cluff

Get On With It

Unsung Heroes

CONTENTS

FOREWORD

Charles Moore

THIS ADMIRABLY SLIM volume is really the last of a trilogy. Avoiding the pomposity and unwieldiness of formal memoirs which burden the author with having to retrace every major aspect of his life, Algy Cluff has crafted a series of short essays and vignettes. They are mainly about other people, but they amount, subtly, to an autobiography.

Algy is a man who, as is often said of leading members of the Royal Family, has touched life at many points. He has been a soldier, businessman and publisher. He knows the life of clubland and of the aristocracy, but also of the practical world, and of how Englishmen behave in far-flung countries, in many of which, particularly in Africa, he has himself mined and drilled. He looks at all these milieus with an original eye. I like very much, for example, his attitude to Britain's colonial history, which manages to be both sympathetic and highly critical at the same time (see the chapter entitled 'The Devonshire Doctrine'). And I love his gift for rescuing from obscurity some interesting figure or unusual tradition. Take his account of Major E. J. P. Cussen, who saved P. G. Wodehouse from the disgrace his own naïveté towards the Nazis had brought upon him, or his opening chapter about the pleasingly pointless 'Bank Picket' now, sadly, defunct.

Too many writers move too much among their own kind. They tend to end up writing about writing and about writers. After a bit, readers are not much interested. Algy is a great reader, and has a lovely, economical literary style, but he writes chiefly about characters unknown to the world of letters. They emerge fresh from these pages – the beautiful, compassionate Sacha Abercorn, the unexpected loyalty of Patrick Lichfield, the tragi-comic fate of Admiral Sir John Kelly, the sweet nature of Angus Ogilvy and the less sweet one of 'Tiny' Rowland. It is always high praise of a writer to say that he depicts worlds in ways that no one else has managed, but it is true of Algy, who has turned to authorship only in his seventies.

For many years, Algy has devoted some of his great energies to helping save war memorials, latterly including The Remembrance Trust, established to restore the graves and monuments of men who died abroad for their country. In his writing, he is himself a great memorialist of unusual customs, places and people – sharp, yet kind; sad, yet funny; modest, unique.

By the Way...

I

The Bank Picket

THE ANTI-PAPACY RIOTS of 1790, the so-called Gordon Riots, included an assault on the Bank of England, which led to calls for the Bank to receive military protection. Accordingly, for the ensuing two hundred years a detachment of Guardsmen commanded by an Ensign (Guards for 2nd Lieutenant) would march out at 6 p.m. every evening from Wellington Barracks to the Bank at Mansion House, returning at 6 a.m. the following morning.

On a number of occasions in the 1960s I was one of those ensigns. It is difficult to appreciate the fact, but London traffic in those days was far more sclerotic than it is now. It was not until Ernest Marples, Minister of Transport, introduced the one-way system that the traffic flow improved. Navigating a platoon of cursing Guardsmen through the late rush-hour grid-lock of the time was something of a challenge for a young officer.

Having arrived at the Bank the Guardsmen began their task of protecting our bullion reserves by patrolling the corridors, whilst the Ensign repaired to a comfortable flat and changed into Mess dress, before dining with a male guest. Dinner was in the Governor's dining room and was served by the staff in their famous pink livery. Red wine followed by port was part of the routine which, since the next day required the detachment to march back at 6 a.m., led to mild hangovers, compounded by the rule that for security reasons no windows were allowed open in the flat.

The return journey was curiously stirring: the streets lay empty and we marched along unimpeded by cars. The route required sent one along the Embankment, into Whitehall and then through the Horse Guards Arch, straight down to Horse Guards Avenue, turning left and then right into Birdcage Walk.

One carefree morning I made a subversive decision to ignore the manual, and instead of marching straight down the Avenue I took a short cut diagonally across Horse Guards Parade Ground. This rash act had an immediate denouement: there was an ancient plane tree from behind which sprang the Regimental Adjutant in full uniform. This was none other than Captain Bernard Gordon Lennox, an officer of undoubted competence but devoid of humour.

'Do that again!' he shouted, and I had no alternative but to wheel my irritated detachment round and back to Horse Guards Arch, where we this time took the prescribed route. This early example of my un-military tendency to think for myself resulted in my commanding the Bank Picket every day for another week.

The Bank Picket was eventually discontinued in 1973; later, of course, and thanks to Gordon Brown's decision to sell most of the country's bullion, the Picket would have anyway become otiose, with nothing left to guard.

***

I had a social connection with the Bank of England through my friendship with two senior officials, John Waddell-Dudley (with whose son I had been at school and who was, I believe, at one time the Chief Cashier), and with an amazing character, Bernard Rickatson-Hatt. He had joined the Bank after a distinguished career at Reuters. His dress for work, as with many others then, was black jacket, striped trousers, bowler hat and rolled umbrella topped off, in

Bernard's case, by a monocle and a daily carnation. I expect he would be tasered if he turned up for work so attired today.

Another rather grander connection was with Rowley, Earl of Cromer, who had been a Grenadier during the war before joining the family bank, Barings. He then served rather uneasily as the Bank of England Governor whilst Harold Wilson was Prime Minister, before being appointed our Ambassador to the United States. After that posting he returned briefly to Barings, before becoming a tax exile in Jersey – rather an unusual choice for a former Bank of England Governor. I am friendly with his son Evelyn, also a tax exile. Barings were in the 1970s the bankers to Cluff Oil during the early days of the North Sea Oil saga and I am much in their debt for the confidence they showed by raising the money to drill our first well, which became the Buchan Oil Field. In particular I remember with affection and respect Derek MacLennan, shy and cautious, and Charles Williams, an alumnus of Westminster, socialist, intellectual, cricketer and biographer who later became a Labour peer in the House of Lords. He married the admirable Jane, who was for many years Secretary of The Other Club, after serving as one of Winston Churchill's wartime secretaries. Derek MacLennan alas died young.

The Other Club is a dining club, founded in 1911 by Winston Churchill and F. E. Smith as a consequence of them both being blackballed by The Club! The Other Club was held in high regard by Churchill, who attended virtually every dinner until his death. Jane is the mother of the present Archbishop of Canterbury, who strangely served at one point as the Finance Director of Enterprise Oil, a North Sea production company.

Derek once asked me to lunch at Barings with my then Finance Director, a clever but egregious fellow, Daniel Lux. We were chatting to Rowley Cromer before lunch who said:

'What you need is a cash flow.'

To my horror I heard Lux reply: 'We have one, we have a rights issue every year.'

'That is not what I meant,' his lordship replied, turning his back on us.

A rights issue, a common enough practice, is a process that involves offering new shares to existing shareholders for cash. To mention it would not have impressed this titan of the banking world, who was thinking more in line of cash flow being generated by the profitability of the company!

***

The Barings demise ranks as one of the most astonishing financial events of my lifetime. My friends at the Bank of England had long since departed the scene, but I know one individual who was present on the dismal weekend when a rescue was discussed at a meeting convened by the then Governor, Eddie George. Although the position was hopeless he told me that Barings' case was not helped by the executives giving the impression that they were more concerned to protect their own bonuses than they were for the future of Barings Bank. One gallant exception to this was Peter Norris, who did not seek to evade his share of the blame and has happily gone on to another successful career with Branson.

I recall discussing some previous banking scandals with Geoffrey Barnett, another Barings director, a frugal and decent man, who terminated the conversation by saying 'Of course nothing like that could happen at Barings.' Three weeks later it did. It was particularly hard for Geoffrey to bear as he had no responsibility for the fiasco and, indeed, was a model Director General of the Takeover Panel.

2

HMS *CURACOA*

THERE HAVE, I believe, been at various times three HMS *Curacoa*s in the Royal Navy, but I am concerned with the last one, a light cruiser launched in 1919. She made a tragi-comic contribution to naval folklore at the funeral at sea of Admiral of the Fleet Sir John Kelly, but there was nothing comic about her demise in 1942.

Sir John Kelly was a popular man below deck as well as being a favourite of King George V and a thoroughly competent officer. In 1931 Ramsay MacDonald's Government imposed a 10 per cent cut in naval pay, which immediately prompted the so-called Invergordon Mutiny of the Atlantic Fleet (subsequently the Home Fleet). This mutiny involved most Royal Navy ships and led to recriminations against the Admiralty and certain naval officers for their cack-handed management of the situation. Admiral Kelly, well known by the sailors to be sympathetic to their cause, was offered command of the entire Fleet immediately after the humiliating mutiny, which he accepted on the condition that over three hundred 'troublemakers' were transferred out of the Fleet to shore positions. Kelly rapidly revived the Fleet's morale but exhausted himself in the process, prompting his retirement and death in 1936. A grateful country honoured him with a State Funeral at St Martin-in-the-Fields; his coffin was then transferred by train to Portsmouth and placed aboard HMS *Curacoa* prior to a burial at sea.

On board, alongside the Admiral's family, was a fleet of twenty Admirals, as well as courtiers and many other diplomatic and naval dignitaries. The Admiral's coffin, after a short passage, was committed to the deep. However, instead of sinking gently to the seabed the coffin resolutely remained afloat, to the embarrassment of the distinguished company and to the distress of the gallant Admiral's family, who were promptly ushered below deck.

Seldom, if ever, had such a maritime problem held the attention of so many Admirals as did the case of the floating coffin. After some indecision the crafty Admirals determined that the only solution, other than towing the coffin back to shore, was to open fire with HMS *Curacoa*'s

3-inch guns. The order was duly given, but the coffin, drifting away from the ship, proved a challenging target for the gunnery detachment and it was only after thirty minutes that the intense bombardment succeeded in reducing the coffin to firewood, releasing the poor Admiral to the embrace of the sea. Thereafter, when distinguished Admirals were committed to burial at sea, ballast, usually of exploded shell cases, was included.

***

HMS *Curacoa*, a ship of some 4,000 tonnes, carried out routine convoy and anti-aircraft duties, until in October 1942 she was involved in one of the most shocking maritime events of the last war, which not only resulted in massive loss of life (despite no enemy ships being involved) but which also raised important questions of competence, as well as moral questions of responsibility.

The grim circumstances arose when HMS *Curacoa*, commanded by her Captain, J. W. Boutwood DSO RN, was on convoy duties north of the Irish coast. The two Cunard liners *Queen Mary* and *Queen Elizabeth* had been requisitioned as troopships in 1942, their principal role being to ferry around twenty thousand American soldiers a time from New York to Southampton. They had been repainted gunmetal grey and could maintain 25 knots (30 miles per hour) as their engines drove the 40,000-tonne leviathans through the ocean, all the time zig-zagging in order to confuse German submarines. In fact their speed was such that no submarine could match it.

On 2nd October the *Queen Mary*, with a complement of ten thousand troops, was twenty miles off the Irish coast when HMS *Curacoa* was instructed to join the Southampton-bound convoy. Precisely why the resulting disaster occurred is unclear: as the *Curacoa's* ageing engines strove to accompany the *Queen Mary* a serious error of command and seamanship unfolded, perhaps on the bridge of both ships, which resulted in the *Queen Mary* colliding at full speed with the *Curacoa*, literally slicing her in two. Three hundred and eighty-five sailors were either killed on impact or pitched into the icy and oil-covered sea. The horror of their wretchedness was compounded by the sight of the *Queen Mary* continuing on her course, at a reduced speed of ten knots, having suffered severe damage. What thoughts of despair and fury must have tortured the drowning sailors as they realised they were being abandoned. A destroyer, HMS *Barham*, is recorded as having picked up ninety survivors, ten of whom expired before they covered the twenty miles to the Irish coast. It is thought three hundred men were drowned. There was no reference to the tragedy until four years later when a court of enquiry was convened.

It emerged that Captain Illingworth of the Cunard line, who was in command of the *Queen Mary*, had instructions that his ship was not to deviate from her course and purpose, regardless of circumstances. This was in respect of the submarine menace and the need to maintain full speed. But the collision rendered the *Queen Mary* unable to achieve more than ten knots. Could he not have had the humanity to help the crew of the ship that he had sunk? Illingworth must have faced one of the greatest moral dilemmas imaginable. After the war Illingworth was knighted and the Admiralty sued Cunard for damages to their ship (not for the families of the drowned mariners).

The House of Lords eventually upheld a ruling that shared culpability, though no discussion of the moral issues ensued. A horrific tale in which the heroes mostly died.

3

Patrick Lichfield

IT WAS IN the Army in 1961 that I met Patrick Anson, as he was before succeeding his grandfather to the title in 1960, his father having died in 1958. His mother, born a Bowes-Lyon and therefore rendering Patrick a cousin of the Royal Family, had married Prince George of Denmark, a genial officer in the Danish Army and for many years the Danish Defence Attaché to London.

We were in the 1st Battalion of the Grenadier Guards, which was then stationed at Kandahar Barracks in Tidworth. I had originally joined the 3rd Battalion in 1959 at Wellington Barracks and I had the melancholy task of jointly carrying the Battalion's Colours to be laid to rest in the Guard's Chapel when the 3rd Battalion evaporated in one of the sporadic defence cuts. The 1st Battalion, which included the elite Queen's Company, was commanded by the intellectual and aristocratic David Fraser, who to no one's surprise eventually became a full

General and, after his retirement, a military historian of consequence. It is no disparagement of his considerable abilities to say that, if he were lacking anything, it is what we now characterise as 'people skills'. No liberties were taken with him, despite his tendency to deliver himself in the Officers' Mess of portentous sentences beginning 'Far be it for me to be complacent about Communist China...' or 'I wish to command in a theatre of war and do battle with a worthy opponent...' He had a moustache and prominent teeth and ended his pronouncements with a sibilant hiss, but we hung on every word, although contributing little to the conversation other than 'Yes, Colonel David' or 'Of course, Colonel David'. He was complemented as adjutant by a fine and fierce figure, David Fanshawe, irreverently known as 'Fanbelt'. Both had a twinkle in the eye, however, and we younger officers became very fond of and loyal to both.

Ironically, and little understood today, a high degree of discipline actually serves to bring out a corresponding degree of humour and pride. We were indeed very proud of our regiment and laughter became the antidote to discipline. The Intelligence Officer was none other than my friend Patrick, and with his ready wit and charm he was a perfect foil to Colonel David's austere manner. Life accordingly was harmonious at Kandahar Barracks, although some of the younger officers, including Lichfield (which he became in 1960), were seized by a deranged determination to drive to London (seventy-five miles) whenever possible. Nicholas Villiers, another contemporary, was the leader of this congeries, for whom the opposite sex was the real challenge in life. Other officers – John ('Cat's Eyes' … he could see in the dark) Semple, James Cheetham, John Magnay and I – preferred the peace and companionship of the Officers' Mess, presided over by the ample figure of Sergeant Speke.

All this terminated when the Battalion was directed to the then British Cameroons in West Africa, where a plebiscite was about to be held in which the citizens were to be given the choice of merging with either Nigeria or the French Cameroons. Independence was not an option. Capriciously they voted to be subsumed into the French Cameroons, notwithstanding that this involved changing their language and legal system. It has not been a success. The 1st Battalion embarked on the troopship *Devonshire* and after a three-week voyage, with stops in Palma and Lagos, we finally arrived in the

Cameroons, a country with few distinguishing features other than boasting the highest rainfall of any African country.

Patrick, as Intelligence Officer, had flown in advance and had missed the delights of the sea voyage. We dispersed in various directions so that our presence was evident throughout the main population centres – Buea (the capital), Kumba, Mamfe and Bamenda. As I have recorded elsewhere (*Get On With It*, 2016) I was detached from the Battalion and charged, along with various drill sergeants, with the task of training the so-called mobile police force.

Patrick was an exemplary Intelligence Officer – bright, un-pompous and popular. Since the Commanding Officer spent a disproportionate amount of time sitting on the lavatory (the climate did not suit everyone) he had to assume more demanding responsibilities than otherwise would have been the case.

***

When we had completed our task in the country we returned to Kandahar Barracks, Colonel David collected his OBE and most of my contemporaries, including Patrick, began to return to civilian life, whereas I signed on with the

Guards Independent Parachute Company, leading to various adventures in Cyprus and Borneo, before leaving the Army myself in 1965.

During the latter part of the 1960s Patrick, Nicholas Villiers, Andrew Parker-Bowles (still also a serving officer in the Royal Horse Guards), Brian Alexander (who had served in his famous father, the Field Marshal's, Regiment – the Irish Guards) together with an altogether more bohemian but benign Irishman, Donough O'Brien, elected to share a flat on the top floor of 42 Wilton Place, then owned by the Savoy Group, itself controlled by Sir Hugh Wontner. Sir Hugh's beautiful daughter, Jennifer, was the subject of the attentions of both Lichfield and Villiers and was prevailed upon to persuade her father to grant a lease to the whole top floor for £6 per week at one week's notice, pending demolition. This arrangement continued until 42 Wilton Place was demolished in the mid 1970s (the site is now the home of the Berkeley Hotel), although Nicholas Villiers still lives 100 yards away in Wilton Crescent.

Patrick had resolved meanwhile to take the then unorthodox career move into photography, and conveniently the ground floor of Wilton Place was then being used as a studio by a professional photographer, Dmitri Kasterine, assisted by Michael Wallis, a true original. Patrick became part of this rather dotty but talented team.

Patrick was evangelical about his chosen profession, and his natural talent, aided by his undoubted charm and connections, served to establish him rapidly as an independent portrait photographer, trading as Patrick Lichfield. He, along with David Bailey, was arguably the leading London portrait photographer for over twenty-five years.

The arresting and unique feature about Patrick, however, was the binary aspect to his life. During the week he was the celebrity photographer, living a successful if rackety existence in London, whilst at the weekend he was Lichfield, the Earl, and held court at the family property in Staffordshire. His photographic fame brought with it significant financial success and enabled him to care for and to expand the Shugborough Estate. I recall him telling me whilst we were at Kandahar Barracks that his father had been a member of a Lloyd's syndicate that had imploded and forced the family to raise funds by selling thousands of acres of Staffordshire. To his great credit, through his photographic competence he was able to buy back this land. How sad it is that within a month of his death his trustees (with one, Hugh Myddelton, dissenting) had sold everything in Staffordshire that he had laboured to preserve.

Notwithstanding his unconventional London life he remained steadfast with regard to his more conventional friends, in particular the equity holders in 42 Wilton Place. Similarly, girlfriends were mainly confined to the society pages and included many of the acknowledged beauties of the time. In 1975, when he was thirty-six, he married Leonora, a sister of the then Duke of Westminster. This marriage terminated in divorce after eleven years, although they had an heir and two daughters.

It is undeniable that the intensity of his professional life led to the emergence of a generic propensity for alcohol and tobacco and caused him to be an erratic, although benevolent, family man. Towards the end of his life he had the good fortune to love and live with Annunziata Asquith, who not only introduced coherence and stability to his life, but also was and is the guardian of his legacy. However, there was nothing she could do to stop the destruction wrought – principally by tobacco – and it was distressing to observe the onset of lung disease.

Patrick was an excellent shot, and many times I had the good fortune to stay at Shugborough for a weekend of shooting; he had created an outstanding partridge shoot there, guided by the steady hand of Major Rodney Haszard, his land agent.

Patrick's sister Elizabeth, who was also married to a photographer, the late Sir Geoffrey Shakerley, played hostess at Shugborough after Patrick's divorce. As is customary on these occasions, before the guests retire for the night they indicate to their hostess what time they would like to be called. We duly conveyed our requests, such as '7.30 and with a cup of tea'. Amongst the party were Princess Anne and her then husband Captain Mark Phillips. Later in the evening I, along with another longstanding friend of Patrick's, Barry Dinan, went into the kitchen looking for a bottle of whisky and observed the morning list, to which Princess Anne's detective had added '12 noon gin and tonic'.

It was at a shoot on the estate of Wafic Said, a Syrian, that tragically Patrick's body was overwhelmed and he died at the wheel of a Land Rover.

Wafic Said once did me the dubious compliment of falling fast asleep whilst I was talking to him at dinner at Blenheim Place – a disconcerting experience about which the book of etiquette remains silent. Do you go on talking as if nothing had happened, wake your audience up or go to sleep yourself in sympathy? I recall doing none of these things, but later asked my wife to advise me – frankly – whether I had in fact become something of a bore.

Patrick's vitality, good humour and genuine capacity for friendship are missed by many. A great concourse was present at the funeral service at Chester Cathedral and at the memorial service at the Guards Chapel. Addresses were given by Nicholas Villiers, Jackie Stewart, Joanna Lumley and myself, recording his duality of personality. Since Patrick was such an amiable snob I elected to read out the letter which Evelyn Waugh wrote to his wife concerning an 'explosion' set off by the Royal Engineers at Lord Glasgow's Scottish estate in 1942 (one of the funniest letters in the English language).

Patrick was not only a highly successful individual, but he was interesting in a metaphysical way, by which I mean that notwithstanding his celebrity and his wealth the most powerful compulsion throughout his life remained his service in the Grenadier Guards. The outward indicator of this, apart from his constant capacity for military reminiscing, included the employment of his father's soldier servant Percy, and subsequently Percy's son Brendan, as his butler, his attachment to his Guards tie (it was the only tie he possessed) and the fact that nearly all his enduring male friendships (in particular Villiers, Parker-Bowles, Alexander, Dinan and myself) were forged during those four years as a Grenadier.

4

BELLA DARVI

IN 1960, WHEN I was a twenty-year-old Ensign in the Grenadier Guards stationed at Chelsea Barracks (now a housing estate), my parents rented a house in Villefranche and invited me and three other young officers to stay. They were George Crawford, a Scots Guard and brother of the animal artist Susan, Johnnie Pascoe, also of the Scots Guards and Jasper Larken, a fellow Grenadier. We drove down to Villefranche in some antique car and had a great time draped around the swimming pool during the day, while in the evenings we sallied forth to the casinos in Beaulieu and Monte Carlo with funds generously provided by my parents.

One evening, before the other three set off for home, we had a farewell dinner in a restaurant called The Pirate before visiting the Casino. I wandered around the chemin de fer tables and suddenly became transfixed by a vision of beauty sitting behind a pile of chips.

I was in love! A friendly waiter revealed that the object of my desire was a film actress called Bella Darvi, that she was staying at the Hôtel de Paris (the most expensive hotel in Monaco) and that she was the current squeeze of Darryl Zanuck, the married American producer. I hopped around from foot to foot as I watched the love of my life gradually reduce the pile of chips in front of her.

The next morning I borrowed some money from my father and dispatched a bouquet of flowers the size of Kew Gardens to the Hôtel de Paris with a note asking her to dinner at Le Pirate. Incredibly she agreed to this. I hired the largest taxi in Monaco and somehow I managed to pay for the dinner as well. The mistaken impression she had that I was an English Croesus, added to my gangling charms, meant the evening progressed well and I got back to my parents' villa at about 4 a.m. without waking them.

I had to fly back to re-join the regiment that day, and was due on Queen's Guard at St James's Palace two days later. I promised La Darvi that I would meet her in Paris the following weekend at the George V. I was there sitting in the foyer, nervously awaiting her arrival, when there was a loud crash outside and the love of my life stormed into the hotel covered in glass and blood, shrieking for a doctor. I retreated behind the newspaper I was reading, and the moment she was in the lift I fled back to the airport.

This proved to be a lucky, if ungentlemanly, escape for my younger self as alas poor Bella was already on a spiral of destruction: mentally unstable and addicted to gambling, she bounced from one rich 'patron' to another, eventually selling her possessions, including her two poodles, to finance her habit. Her life ended tragically in suicide in 1971 at the age of only forty-two.

5

NEW YORK

IN 1966 I unsuccessfully contested the Ardwick Division of Manchester as an unofficial Conservative candidate. I was aged twenty-six and knew very little about anything except the Brigade of Guards and the decolonisation of our Empire, which was in full swing. For this reason I was not included on the official roll of candidates kept by Conservative Central Office. Indeed I never entered that building on Smith Square, although for twenty-seven years I have lived next door to it. The local Association, who were a fairly bloody-minded collection of ladies in hats, together with one obnoxious young man, must have been bamboozled by my enthusiasm as I was unanimously adopted to fight the General Election against the legendary Labour MP Leslie Lever.

I detested canvassing, although I had glamorous assistance from Serena Russell, a statuesque and charming American blonde, whose mother was the sister of Sunny (Duke

27

of) Marlborough. I was keen on Serena but had not the slightest notion of what I really wanted to do after this political episode. My campaign got off to an unfortunate start as my kindly father dropped me off at the constituency office in his Bentley before he drove off to the family office in Dolphin Street. The first morning of this luxurious procedure a local newspaper photographed me alighting from the capitalist chariot and gleefully displayed my plutocratic arrival at the humble constituency office on their front page. Thereafter my father dropped me a good mile away and I attempted to retrieve the situation by apparently walking all the way to work.

The Chairman of the Association was one Walton Lyon, and I was the first Guards officer he had ever met; I presumed the same went for *any* member of the electorate for that matter. Our relationship was always awkward, whereas I hit it off much better with my opponent Leslie Lever. He was so awful that I liked him. All things to all men, he was immensely popular and, Orthodox Jew as he was, proudly wore a Papal decoration. When I attended my first public debate with him he stood up and led the applause and, in his speech, he said he hoped the Conservative Party would find a safe seat for this young man elsewhere. On polling day cars toured the constituency with people with megaphones crying 'All out for Leslie'! In the event there was a 3 per cent swing to the Tories, although Leslie was re-elected with a huge majority.

I recall being rather relieved when it was all over.

As a result of my father's bountifulness I still had no need for employment, so I resolved to spend the rest of 1966 in New York, where my Grenadier and sailing friend, Jasper Larken, had gone to work for a bank. At this time I was loosely associated with the Ionian Bank (proprietors J. M. Trusted and E. M. Behrens). These two, previously stockbrokers, had acquired the Ionian name and hired an engaging and talented team, which was located at 64 Coleman Street in the City.

Although my contribution to the Ionian success was negligible, I forged close friendships there, and when I mentioned that I was planning a visit to New York for six months it was quickly decided that I could present myself as their representative. That, coupled with my credentials as a failed politician, and together with my slim frame, double-breasted suits and

English accent, was sufficient to gain access to Manhattan's social and business world. This I took full advantage of and spent six months in a haze of dry martinis.

Among the first Americans I met and became friendly with was the Ruskin family. I think they were of Russian-Jewish origin and Professor Ruskin had made a fortune from some medical advance. They lived in a huge brownstone house on the Upper East Side, entirely decorated in the Art Deco style. Mrs Ruskin was a large and formidable matron of sharp intelligence, complemented by a very low threshold of boredom. This was manifest when, attending a dinner party and finding the conversation wanting, she would put on her reading glasses, retrieve a novel from her handbag and sit there serenely reading until the end of the meal. Her daughter, Ariane, was an attractive although fragile girl, prematurely grey, with whom I had a brief romance. Professor Ruskin gained heroic status for saving lives from a burning building after even the fire department had given up hope.

After a short while I became friendly with a number of British officials working mostly with the United Nations, including Ralph Townley, John Guinness (who was the Secretary General's personal assistant), David Lane and

Stanley Wright (ex-HM Treasury and Lazard). Guinness had a small apartment at 131 East 66 Street, which he very kindly lent to me for three months when he went travelling with his boss, U Thant.

I also became very friendly with a dear old boy, Sir Senerat Gunewardene, who was the Ceylon (as it was then) representative to the UN Committee on Decolonization, at which the UK got constant abuse, skilfully and urbanely managed by Francis Brown, a Welsh Guards officer, who batted away insults on a daily basis. I used to take Sir Senerat to lunch at a restaurant close by the United Nations Headquarters and put the case for colonisation to him over a bottle of wine and a couple of brandies, by which time he was fully converted and staggered back to the committee room to make some supportive comments about the British Empire, to the amazement of Francis Brown who assumed, correctly, that he had been drinking!

Elsewhere, Nelson Rockefeller was running for re-election as Governor of New York State. My Uncle Willie had lived for fifty years in New York and held court at the architecturally dramatic Metropolitan Club on Fifth Avenue, where he introduced me to a lawyer, Herbert Roth, who was working on the Rockefeller re-election campaign, as well as other races. My only claim to fame was to write the speech that lost the election for one particular Congressman. I then stepped back from 'public' life to advance the course of the Ionian Bank in New York, which I fear was not attended by much success either. On my part, however, I owe a debt to the Ionian as they had the imagination and judgement to realise the potential that the North Sea offered and, under the direction of Sam Hamburger and the clever, if laconic, Christopher (Inky) Brett, set up Oil Exploration Holdings to participate in North Sea licences. I was much interested by this, and indeed was so intrigued by it all that I promptly left the Ionian Bank and founded my own oil company.

6

WEST-END CHARACTERS

CLUBS DO DEFINE their members, although not perhaps as drastically as suggested by Evelyn Waugh and recounted by Anthony Powell: Powell once introduced Waugh to a third party and happened to add that he was a member of the Travellers Club.

'Oh, I didn't know you were homosexual,' said Waugh.

Incidentally, Anthony Powell's character Widmerpool is supposedly based on a member of the St James's Club – an uncharacteristically boorish member. The St James's undoubtedly boasted the most eccentric members until its untimely and unnecessary demise in the 1960s. Just a cursory reflection on long-dead members produces an uncompromising reaction:

Ivor Pakenham and Lawrence Gresley – obnoxious, Sir Leigh Ashton – crackers, Nico Tollenaar ('The Flying Dutchman' as he walked with difficulty) – rich, Nubar Gulbenkian – very

rich, Lord Stonor – mad, Loopy Whitbread –
raving mad, Andrew Bowring – drunk … and
so on.

I often wondered how half of them managed
to get dressed in the morning. The staff were
just as batty, with the distinguished exception of
Johnny Macrea, the barman. The two excellent
Irish porters, O'Donnell and Paddy, were both
understood to be fully paid-up members of the
IRA, O'Donnell having the rank of General.

One of my most memorable clubland events
was Richard King's sixtieth birthday at Boodle's,
which I had arranged in the lovely saloon. The
party was attended by many ornaments of the
time including Ted Dexter, Barry Humphries,
Teddy Goldsmith (Jimmy's estimable brother)
and numerous golfing QCs from Sunningdale.
Paddy Pakenham proposed the toast, men-
tioning everyone in the room except Richard,
before clambering on the table and singing the
Argentine National Anthem (this was during
the Falklands War). He was removed from the
building by the Secretary and staff still in full
voice.

A year later I risked giving another dinner
there on Paddy's birthday, which gave me
the opportunity of thanking him for all the
hospitality he had dispensed to me over the

preceding twenty-five years (one lunch at a dive next to the Old Bailey, after which I got food poisoning!).

Although I am not a member of the Royal Wimbledon Golf Club, my friends Richard King and Michael Haines both had contrasting experiences there. Richard, playing golf as a guest, was relieving himself in a washbasin when he was interrupted by an elderly gentleman who began protesting loudly.

'Don't worry, I'm playing with a member...' responded Richard.

Michael Haines, a distinguished accountant, was sitting drinking in the bar after playing eighteen holes. This was in the days of fixed times for drinking under the absurd old licensing laws. Unknown to Michael and the other accountants, judges and bankers also in there after hours, a zealous new constable had been appointed to the area. It was well known that 'out-of-hours' drinking occurred there, so he decided to strike. Materialising in the bar to the consternation of those present, he moved round the room taking particulars of the distinguished and elderly miscreants. Finally it was Michael's turn.

'What is your address, age and occupation?' the constable intoned, 'and what beverages are you drinking?' To which Michael replied: 'Oh that's very kind of you officer, I'll have a large gin and tonic please!'

One of the more agreeable fellow officers in the 3rd Battalion Grenadier Guards, with whom I served at Wellington Barracks through the summer of 1960, was Captain David Bigelow Dodge. He radiated good humour, but being devoid of ambition disappeared without trace after he left the Army in 1963. In fact he lived quietly in Devonshire and I never saw him again. Had I been more inquisitive, or had he been less modest, I would have realised that he was not only a scion of American aristocracy but that he was the son of the 'Dodger': Colonel John Bigelow Dodge, DSO, DSC, MC. His father, the Colonel, is sadly forgotten now, but really was a remarkable man, paramount in the annals of escapology and brave and resolute in both the First and Second World Wars. He was the real hero of the events that inspired the film *The Great Escape*, and was famously portrayed by Steve McQueen.

Born in New York in 1894 of the founding family of the Phelps Dodge copper dynasty, John Bigelow Dodge joined the RNR Division as a sub-lieutenant immediately on the outbreak of the war in 1914. He served at Antwerp and Gallipoli and, transferring to the Army, in France. He was awarded the DSC in 1915 for gallantry and the DSO in France where, aged twenty four, he commanded the 16th Battalion of the Royal Sussex Regiment. To have been decorated in the Army and the Navy was some sort of record, but nothing to compare with the award of the Military Cross in the Second World War aged fifty-one, having unsuccessfully escaped five times after being captured at St Valery in 1940. He is, I believe, the oldest man to have been awarded that medal.

Between the two wars he was a stockbroker in the City of London and always an idealist. He made a number of unsuccessful attempts to gain election to Parliament, although he was elected to the London County Council for Mile End 1921–31. Incongruously, he died whilst hailing a taxi in the West End in 1960. Like his son David he had a most attractive manner and was very much a clubman all his life, including membership of White's and the Royal Yacht Squadron.

His amazing exploits were recorded in a biography, *The Dodger* by Tim Carroll, in 1990.

7

Sam White, Aspers and Jimmy Goldsmith

IN 1980 THE time seemed propitious for the careers of certain larger-than-life characters, in particular Sir Jimmy Goldsmith and John Aspinall (Aspers). Jimmy was always kind and courteous to me and his courtesy was never corroded by his celebrity. Goldsmith, Jim Slater, James Hanson and Gordon White thrived in those pre-regulatory days and though their activities – largely asset stripping – would be rendered impossible today, nonetheless there was something full-blooded and dashing about them, especially when compared to the smug, secretive world of private equity and hedge fund practices today. Capitalism then was unfettered, and many bovine and complacent corporate household names succumbed to the relentless energy of the new entrepreneurs. Interestingly one common factor seemed to obtain amongst the most successful new men – they had no university education. Be they old

Etonians (Goldsmith) or non-public-school boys (Hanson, John King, White, Slater, 'Tiny' Rowland etc.) none had apparently wasted three or four years of their lives getting a degree. The universities now no longer disdain commerce, but the introduction of stifling business regulation has led to the birth of a huge population of non-productive apparatchiks. Their existence seems to have done nothing to eradicate real criminality, but just added another layer of spurious non-criminality to the long, long list of controls. It sounds irrelevant, but so much legislation has been introduced (mostly, ironically, by Thatcher) that it has become necessary to break at least one footling law a day in order to maintain one's self-respect! These are not 'laws', they are 'restrictions'.

The Bribery Act is another nail in the UK entrepreneurial coffin, piloted through Parliament by a decent but, in my view, misguided politician – Jack Straw. Not only is it insulting in that it is implicit that businessmen have a tendency to be corrupt, but the unintended consequences include that Non-Executive Directors have become dead hands on Boards of Directors: rightly concerned that they may face prosecution for minor transactions of which they are unaware.

***

Feeding on the old unrestricted capitalism were the hyenas of capitalism – the gambling fraternity. Paramount, if that is the correct word, amongst them was John Aspinall. Whatever effect he had it was impossible in that decade to ignore him. Although I was never a gambler (at least whilst out of office hours), I became very friendly with Aspers and was a neighbour of his, my clifftop house being close both to Howletts and to Port Lympne. It was at the latter, a Herbert Baker-designed house overlooking the Romney Marsh, that a magnificently louche ball was given by Aspers in May 1980. I was asked if I could have a number of Aspers' friends to stay for the ball weekend. 'They' were Sunny Marlborough, Alexander Hesketh (and his wife, Claire), my then girlfriend Nikkie Howarth and Sam White.

Sam was perhaps a surprise choice, being poor, Jewish, Australian and (previously) Communist. However, on the plus side he certainly was not a bore! Sam held some sort of record, being awarded the OBE for services to journalism whilst remaining a fully paid-up member of the Australian Communist Party. He had been a reporter in Paris, and at the end of the war he was hired by the *Evening Standard* as a foreign correspondent. In those days all newspapers had a correspondent in Paris, Washington, Hong Kong and Johannesburg. Sam spoke not one word of French (although his wife did) but that was no impediment to his extraordinary success. He had no office and no secretary and for ten years held court in the bar of the Crillon Hotel, and for another ten in the bar of the Travellers Club on the Champs-Élysées. He sat every evening at the same table at the entrance to the elegant courtyard.

Two of Sam's closest friends were Jimmy Goldsmith and his brilliant brother Teddy. They were the sons of Anglo-French Jewish aristocrat Major Frank Goldsmith, and had both been sent to Eton, which institution made little, or in Jimmy's case no, impression on their waywardness. Teddy, ahead of his time, founded the *Ecologist Magazine* and evangelised on the subject throughout his useful and mildly dotty life. He had married a beautiful and lively English girl. After they were divorced I developed a passion for her. One Saturday I asked her to lunch at Au Fin Bec in Soho and judged that I was progressing satisfactorily to an afternoon of romance. However, the restaurant had a series of banquettes, behind which was a platform linking them to the wall. There suddenly appeared a giant rat on this platform – the ex-Mrs Goldsmith screamed and levitated horizontally out of the restaurant, leaving me with the rat, no food and no sex. I never saw her again.

Sam's column, 'Sam White's diary', was a brilliant interpretation of life in Paris and of French politics (largely incomprehensible at this time), complemented by sharp observations on the activities of the French upper classes. Sam became friendly with Jimmy, who put him up for membership of the Travellers, and by association with Aspers, hence his presence at the ball and at my house. Sam was transfixed by the clifftop view of the sea and spent hours staring at it when he was not hurtling around the byways of Kent in Hesketh's 'two seater'. They were rather an incongruous couple but hit it off.

When Sam was struggling with his health (fifty cigarettes a day takes its toll) a friend of his, Christopher Moorsom, asked me if I would commission a portrait of Sam by a certain Russian artist, which would be presented to his beloved Travellers Club. In the event I commissioned two, one for the club, for which I was unthanked, and the other for myself. I did not much take to mine, which featured Sam tieless and casual, whereas he was always in fact very dapper. Hence it remained unhung, lying against a wall in a corridor in my house. One day in passing I decided on a whim to turn the painting to face the wall; the next morning, rather eerily, I had a call from his wife reporting that Sam had sadly died during the night.

Sam was a lovely man and larger than life, as were so many of the Second World War correspondents, such as Alan Moorehead, René Cutforth, Alexander Clifford and Geoffrey Keating. I believe that the other portrait of Sam still hangs in the Travellers Club, keeping a watchful eye over its members.

***

I saw a lot of Aspers in the 1980s. I remember once being asked to lunch at Howletts to meet the film actor James Stewart, after which we were to join our host in the tiger and gorilla cages. Brigadier General Stewart (which rank he had in the USAAF in the Second World War) and Captain Cluff declined this opportunity to show their valour and bravery! When Aspers bought Port Lympne I lent him an oil painting of a buffalo by Terence Cuneo, which his son, Damian, has generously just returned to me forty-five years later.

Dinner in the Clermont Club days was always entertaining, although it was like being in the congregation of a church listening to an address from a sixteenth-century divine in the pulpit. As his hour of dining got later and later I saw much less of Aspers. He was a most unusual man, gifted when young with exceptional looks and a brain to match, which he curiously directed to a destructive purpose, gambling, although defined by a worthy objective, conservation. Does the end justify the means? As noted in one obituary: '... in the various gaming clubs he had run over the years, he had probably done more than Karl Marx to bring about the redistribution of wealth and the ruination of the rich.'

8

SACHA ABERCORN

A T THE END of the nineteenth century, when gold and diamonds were discovered in what was then known as the Union of South Africa, most of the entrepreneurs, other than Cecil Rhodes (who arrived from Bishop's Stortford), originated from Germany, particularly Frankfurt. They were likelier than not to be Jewish (Oppenheimers, Joels and Barnatos for example). In many respects the real winners were not the miners but the middlemen who took no exploration risk, preferring to buy and sell the commodities.

Arguably the most successful of these was the firm of Wernher, Beit & Co. They were the leading diamond dealing firm for many years. Their success translated into massive monetary fortunes and the inevitable mansions on London's Park Lane. Beit was indeed Jewish and from Frankfurt. Julius Wernher, however, was a flaxen-haired Prussian. How they got together is unknown; they probably met in Frankfurt where Julius was educated, but they certainly forged one of the most rewarding business partnerships of the nineteenth and twentieth centuries. Alfred Beit was a bachelor and was not, as is generally thought, created a Baronet. It was his brother Otto who became the first Beit Baronet and his son Alfred, source of the confusion, was the last Beit Baronet, dying rich but childless in 1974, having endured a brief and unwelcome spasm of celebrity when he and his wife, Clementine, were attacked by Rose Dugdale in the name of the IRA at their grand house, Russborough, in Ireland.

The Beits move out of our story and we focus on Julius Wernher, the stern and handsome partner who did receive a baronetcy in 1905. In addition to the de-rigeur Park Lane mansion, Sir Julius acquired an estate, Luton Hoo in Bedfordshire, and the estate remains in the possession of the family. More importantly he married and – unusually for a South African dynasty (with the exception of the Oppenheimers) – produced an heir, Harold, the third and last Baronet, who inherited the title from his elder brother who died childless. Sir Harold, a gallant man, fought in the First World War and survived to become a successful businessman. He married Zia, a Russian aristocrat who was a direct descendant of both Tsar Nicholas I and the poet Alexander Pushkin, and who was, as one might expect, an original and resolute lady. I met her when I believe she was nearly eighty-five, although all I can recall is listening to her golden retriever playing the piano (after a fashion). Harold and Zia lived a many-faceted and useful life, had a son, who was killed in the war aged twenty-four, and two daughters. Gina married Colonel Harold (Bunny) Phillips, and Myra married Sir David Butter.

Sir Harold, by this time the Chairman of Electrolux, played a major role in the success of the Normandy landings, for which he was appointed Major General. It was, however, as racehorse owners and breeders that the Wernher family was best known. Their eldest daughter provided Harold Phillips with a son, Nicky, and four daughters: Sacha, Fiona, Marita and Tally (Natalia). Tragedy, all too often the handmaiden of privilege, struck. Nicky, tall, handsome and reserved, was engaged in an imaginative commercial venture at Luton Hoo, one of Britain's first business parks. Cash-flow problems arose and he ended his life rather than reveal the extent of the problems to his family and friends. He was married to an intelligent

Austrian girl, Lucy Czernin, who bore him two children.

All the daughters are unsurprisingly endowed with character and beauty as well as many other attributes. They are a most unusually talented dynasty, the intellectual and artistic strength of their Russian ancestor Pushkin being most manifest in the extraordinary talent of Marita. The climax of her career thus far occurred at the Grange Park Opera production of *Pushkin*, for which she wrote the libretto, with music by Konstantin Boyarsky. Described as 'brilliant' by Mark Ronan, the conclusion of the performance led to a standing ovation and a round of applause from the cast – the absolute in terms of professional accolade.

Sacha married James, 5th Duke of Abercorn; Fiona, James Burnett of Leys, a Scottish landowner; Marita married Randall Crawley and Tally, the 6th Duke of Westminster. Randall Crawley was similarly blessed with outstanding physical beauty complemented by a remarkable sporting talent. He and his equally accomplished brother, Andrew, both perished in a private plane crash in Italy. Both Marita and Andrew's wife Sarah were pregnant at the time. Eventually they both married again and very happily. Marita to Andrew Knight, variously

Editor of *The Economist* and Chief Executive of *The Telegraph*, and Sarah to a distinguished American mining executive, Hank Slack.

The other sisters, whose Russian ancestry is manifest from their appearance, have made a dignified and unselfish contribution to the community. Tally, an exemplary and strikingly beautiful Duchess in Cheshire, and Fiona an equally successful chatelaine of the House of Burnett in Scotland. Sacha, the eldest daughter, gained heroic status in Northern Ireland, where she worked indefatigably with her husband, never flinching during the worst of the Troubles.

Although not herself an intellectual, Sacha was governed by a combination of philosophical curiosity and natural introspection which found its expression in the writing of Jung. This did not lead to any selfish form of mental examination so much as a determination to be unselfish – as exemplified by her constant dedication to the cause of education in Northern Ireland and, indeed, the overall cause of peace.

Tragically, as I write Sacha has succumbed to cancer, which was identified in March 2018, and after a valiant struggle she died at the end of that year. She will be remembered by many for her courage, kindness and ethereal beauty. During her illness she was cared for with touching devotion by her husband, her children and her siblings.

9

Major E. J. P. Cussen

WHEN THE WAR started P. G. Wodehouse and his formidable wife Ethel were living at Low Wood, their bungalow near Le Touquet. For whatever reason they did not make it across the Channel and when the German Army arrived Wodehouse was eventually arrested (being fifty-nine years old) and interned in various camps before being released from prison, but not from Germany, when he was sixty. Wodehouse was prevailed upon by the German authorities, whilst still interned, to broadcast to his many American readers. This he unwisely did, describing life in a prisoner of war camp as not dissimilar to life in an English public school. Not only did he agree to make five broadcasts, but he allowed himself to be paid for them. These broadcasts caused a storm of protest and indignation in Britain, severely discomforting the hapless Wodehouse, who lived out the remaining two years of the war either staying in some luxury in the Adlon, the best hotel in Berlin, or with an aristocratic anti-Nazi family, the Bodenhausens, in the Hartz mountains, where they were immensely kind to him. The liberation of Paris in 1944 found the Wodehouses in another five-star hotel in Paris.

The broadcasts had naturally come to the attention of MI5, and certain politicians had taken a very strong anti-Wodehouse line, in some cases calling for Wodehouse to be repatriated to Britain and put on trial for treason. Prominent amongst these were Duff Cooper, Quintin Hogg and even Winston Churchill himself, who surprisingly and incredibly seems not only never to have read a Wodehouse novel, but also to have disapproved of Wodehouse the man.

In this febrile atmosphere it is quite possible to entertain the ghastly thought that P. G. Wodehouse, rightly one of the most celebrated authors of the twentieth century, could have been tried for treason and executed. Evelyn Waugh and George Orwell both gallantly spoke up for him, but nonetheless he was in a most vulnerable position when MI5 elected to conduct their own investigation and dispatched to Paris one Major E. J. P. Cussen. A pre-war criminal prosecutor, Cussen was a man of some consequence, although no celebrity. He had been a diligent MI5 officer throughout the war and frequent reference is made to him in *The Diaries of Guy Liddell*, edited by Nigel West. (Liddell was the deputy head of MI5 for most of the war.) After the war Cussen was one of the UK's prosecuting counsels at the Nuremberg war crimes trials, before being appointed a Judge. He died in 1973.

So, in September 1944 Cussen was sent to Paris, charged by MI5 with the task of interviewing Wodehouse and his wife and determining whether there existed sufficient evidence to justify an arrest and eventual prosecution for treason.

It is well recorded that Major Cussen spent a week in Paris in 1944 executing this task. Although Cussen never published an auto-biography it is clear that he was baffled by Wodehouse. However, the conclusion of his investigation, whilst critical of Wodehouse, was that a jury would find it difficult to convict him of an intention to assist the enemy. Cussen strongly advised Wodehouse to 'stay out of the jurisdiction', advice which was repeated by another MI5 officer, Malcolm Muggeridge, who befriended the Wodehouses in Paris, and also by Raymond Needham KC, a distinguished barrister friend of Wodehouse.

In 1947 Sir Hartley Shawcross, the Attorney-General in the Attlee Government, confirmed that there was no guarantee that Wodehouse would not be prosecuted if he returned to the UK, and similar advice was offered by David Maxwell-Fyffe, the Home Secretary, in 1952. Churchill before the end of the war minuted Duff Cooper 'we would prefer not ever to hear about him again…'

Cussen's report was scandalously not released by MI5 until 1980, by which time both Cussen and Wodehouse were dead. However, it is clear that Cussen's wisdom and common-sense advice saved many people's favourite author from execution or imprisonment, and for that we should be grateful to Judge Cussen.

10

THE DEVONSHIRE DOCTRINE

WHEN HAROLD MACMILLAN delivered his notorious 'Wind of Change' speech in Cape Town in February 1960, he provided the catalyst for nationalism in Africa. In point of fact he had used exactly the same phrase in Ghana on 9th January at the start of his African tour, but then the phrase attracted no notice. A similar expression had been used in 1934 by Baldwin in the context of Indian independence, when he had said 'there is a wind of nationalism and freedom blowing round the world and blowing as strongly in Asia as anywhere in the world.' My friend Professor David Dilks has also pointed out that both Sir Jack Johnston and Sir David Hunt (UK High Commissioners in Africa at the time) had claimed, although in no boastful sense, to have suggested 'The Wind of Change' formulation to Macmillan.

In any event his antagonists were shocked, as though Macmillan had *invented* nationalism in Africa, whereas he was merely stating a fact. Cynics maintained that what he really meant was 'Britain is broke and we are getting out of here', and there is an element of truth in this argument, but there was another dimension – the arrival in power of de Gaulle, and the bitter civil war in Algeria. De Gaulle offered virtually all the French possessions in sub-Saharan Africa immediate independence, which understandably had an effect in the British territories there. Macmillan always contended correctly that the British consideration of independence was not a matter of weakness or even economic stringency. Once we had offered independence to India and Asia we were bound to follow in Africa.

To be fair to Macmillan, it was as far back as 1923 that the Duke of Devonshire, the Tory Colonial Secretary of the day, issued a famous but alas forgotten declaration, known as 'The Devonshire Doctrine', that made it abundantly clear that it was the intention of the British Government in any conflict of interest between the African and the white community to always regard the interest of the African as paramount. This had the full support of Bonar Law's Cabinet, and the doctrine of African paramountcy was never challenged until the difficulties arose with white settlers in the 1960s. Interestingly, that Duke of Devonshire was Harold Macmillan's father-in-law.

Within weeks of Macmillan's speech, the wind of change rapidly became a hurricane, and yet at the first Lancaster House African Conference in London on Kenya, in 1960, so little understanding of the urgency existed that the African delegates were issued with passes to the building but not to the conference itself. Kenya's chief representative, Peter Koinange, at the time a milkman in Watford, was the subject of a quatrain by the Permanent Under-Secretary at the Colonial Office, Sir Hilton Poynton.

Mau mau milkman, have you any pass
Yes sir, yes sir, but only Third Class
Good for the cloakroom and good for the loo
But not for the main room among the chosen few.

It is largely forgotten now how deep the divisions were over these moves towards accepting African nationalism, and how complicated the process of pressing ahead became. Reconciling the views of the white settlers in Kenya and Rhodesia was nightmare enough, particularly as the decent white politician Sir Roy Welensky and many of the whites were not actually opposed to the Devonshire Doctrine, but rather genuinely believed that the time had not yet arrived.

We can now see that the speed of political advance in Africa completely overwhelmed the administrative preparations. Africanisation was proceeding, but painfully slowly, and was lagging far behind the constitutional developments. Macmillan's Government was determined not to lose the political momentum, although Ian Macleod told me many years later that the process should have taken twenty years, not two.

What Harold Macmillan wearily called the African maze was in reality a maddening distraction from serious economic issues at home, not to mention de Gaulle's veto of the UK's attempt to join Europe, the Cold War and the Cuban Missile Crisis. One of the great ironies of this period was the huge expenditure of time and debate spent on decolonising Africa and the Far East as rapidly as possible, whilst South Africa was engaged in precisely the reverse policy.

You will find in the final volume of Macmillan's memoirs only two references to South Africa. Both concerned the necessity of dispensing with that country as the only means of preserving the Commonwealth. The word 'apartheid', surely one of the most indefensible crimes of the twentieth century, receives no mention. What did the Commonwealth or the United Nations do about apartheid? Nothing at all.

It is interesting to reflect what the history of South Africa might have been had Field Marshal Smuts won that critical election in 1948. There may not have emerged the perfect solution, but there would have surely been no apartheid. However, for thirty years there was visited on the South African blacks a humiliation and a deprivation of outrageous degree. When de Klerk bowed to the inevitable there were naturally many doomsters on hand contending that a peaceful transition to democracy was impossible. But peaceful it was, and not only that, but the elections were followed by the virtual evaporation of the right-wing Afrikaner as a political force.

***

The British Army mission to the British Cameroons of 1960, in which I served (see Chapter 3), was entirely consistent with the mood of the time. We were there to keep order for the plebiscite, but both options on offer to the citizens (a merger with the much larger French Cameroons or with Nigeria) were unsatisfactory. They chose the French Cameroons and became The Cameroon Republic – but it was rapid and arrogant housekeeping by Britain, whose anxiety was to exit from a problem sideways rather than face it head on.

So, in the space of two or three years, the British, the French, the Spanish and the Portuguese contrived to deliver independence to dozens of countries. But what is independence if it is not supported by universities and economic power? I will tell you – it is a chimera, a 'terrifying but non-existent thing' according to my dictionary. It would naturally be foolish to be overly critical of countries like Britain for frantically seeking to avoid more of those colonial wars, such as we conducted in Malaya, in Cyprus and in Kenya, but the historians of the future will surely excoriate the colonial powers for granting independence without its handmaidens: institutional structures and commercial ownership.

Young, intelligent Africans are now being properly trained and are trying to raise the continent's ethical standards. These youngsters realise that there is no point in political power unless it is complemented by commercial power.

The Anglo-Saxon colonial grip on commerce and mining has eroded, only to be replaced by Chinese, Indian and Russian neo-colonialism. At least the Anglo-Saxon variety carried with it a duty of benign government, whereas contemporary colonialism is a matter of self-interest only. The severity or importance of this issue naturally varies from country to country. In Burkina Faso, for example, there never was a land-owning white elite, and in many of the West African countries where there were large foreign vested interests, such as Unilever and British American Tobacco, the ownership issue never arose because wisely those companies gave the plantations to the people whilst guaranteeing to purchase the produce.

During the thirty years that I operated in Africa I have always been treated courteously, have never paid or been asked for a bribe (except by an Englishman), and never lost one day in industrial action at mines in Ghana or Zimbabwe. I am proud of what was achieved in Africa by the British and how correctly and professionally those colonies were run by unselfish officials possessed of the Devonshire Doctrine: that ultimately the African must be enfranchised. These administrators worked for a pittance in the most difficult conditions and it is time their memory and achievements were celebrated and not mocked.

The irony of Africa has been that one form of colonialism has been replaced by another and little effort has been made to provide Africans with participation in the capitalist protocol. The importance of Stock Exchanges, for example: a means of ensuring corporate governance is observed; a means of moving capital in and out of the continent; and a means of including the African in the process by requiring companies to issue shares to their workforce. I did that myself in Zimbabwe in the 1990s when we listed the shares of our local company on the Harare Stock Exchange, with 15 per cent of the shares being vested in a workers' trust.

Adjutant Captain John Smiley, AC and 3rd Battalion Grenadier Guards rehearse Trooping the Colour, 1960. In the background my Rolls-Royce, bought for £38, which ran out of petrol if driven uphill.

Changing the Guards, AC carrying the Colour behind Major Lord Erskine.

HMS *Curacoa*.

Shugborough – the location of many glorious weekends.

Shugborough shooting party. From 2nd left Mark Phillips, Shaun Normanton, Patrick Lichfield, Major Rodney Haszard (centre) and 2nd right AC and Rupert Deen.

Bella Darvi in her second film, *The Egyptian*, 1954.

Convivial dinner with Paddy Pakenham and Brigadier Michael Lee, Harry Cluff not wanting to go to bed.

Charlie Cluff: the Future (aged 17).

Geoffrey Keating and Jimmy Goldsmith.

Lady Zia Wernher
with her accompanist.

Sacha Abercorn.

'Paddy Pakenham singing the
Argentine National Anthem at
Richard King's birthday at Boodle's.'

Above left: Max Kraan, heroic Dutch-man, outside our office, Bulawayo.

Above: Nicholas Phillips on a tin dredger, Malaysia 1982.

Ronald Winston.

Conrad Black.

Deep in conversation, 11th Duke of Devonshire and Charles Letts in Hong Kong.

Hong Kong delegation at No. 10 lunching with John Major.

Philip Cluff's Godparents: Paddy, Simon Murray, Nana Rawlings, Blondel, Richard King, AC, Diana Seymour and Sunny Marlborough.

Army film and photographic unit, Christmas Day, Arras, 1939. Back row: Philby (third from left) and Sir Robert Mackenzie (sixth from left). Others include the future Field Marshal 'Tiger' Templer and General Mason-MacFarlane, Director of Military Intelligence.

Kim Philby and Sir Robert Mackenzie: 'The night they met!!'

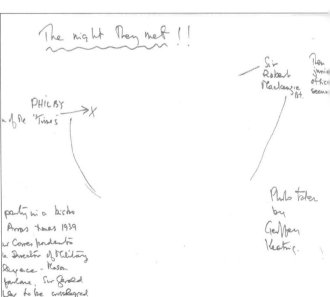

11

HARLEY DRAYTON AND
ANGUS OGILVY

IN THE 1950s and 1960s there flourished
in the City of London a certain Harley
Drayton of 117 Old Broad Street. From
this office he directed the affairs of a number
of investment trusts known as The Old Broad
Street Group, and his name lived on until rela-
tively recently as 'The Drayton Group of Fund
Managers'. Photographs reveal Harley Drayton
as a florid-faced figure with the then widely
worn adornments of double-breasted waistcoat, heavy watch-chain and red carnation. He
lived at Plumpton Hall near Bury St Edmunds,
other than which his *Who's Who* entry for 1952
reveals nothing beyond a long list of directorships. There is no personal information at
all – no date of birth, no place of education,
no reference to his marital status or education.
There is nothing mysterious about his list of
directorships, however – railway companies
(in South America, including Antofagasta);

publishing companies; engineering companies (British Electric Traction); United Newspapers; the Midland Bank and many others. Not listed, however, was a company which proved to be the nemesis of one of his most able lieutenants, Angus Ogilvy. That company was London & Rhodesia Mining & Land Company, later known as LONRHO.

Harley Drayton was possessed of a formidable brain and a strong personality, although lacking in any formal education. Indeed, he recorded that, notwithstanding that the only book he had ever read was the Bible, Ecclesiastes contained all the principles of finance required for the conduct of a businessman. He had a highly unusual facility for memorising financial data and, too old to enlist, he had spent the war years analysing and absorbing all the information relating to the companies controlled by 117 Old Broad Street. After Lord St Davids, the Chairman, had died, Drayton became the de-facto head of the group. (Here I have drawn on the obituary of Drayton in *The Dictionary of National Biography* by Sir Anthony Welby, senior partner of Cazenove's, stockbrokers.)

Drayton managed the affairs of the Old Broad Street Group not only with ingenuity but also originality, controversially vesting 20 per cent of the funds in support of unlisted companies, a procedure which yielded great benefits. This was the time when finance for international utilities was sourced in the City of London and Drayton backed and directed many such companies – tramways, railways, telegraph and bus companies. Curiously he received no honour. Welby declares no interest in his obituary notice, but doubtless Drayton dispensed much valuable patronage to City stockbrokers during those post-war years. He developed a tendency for hiring old Etonians who served him competently and loyally. Amongst these were Angus Ogilvy and Sir Robert Adeane (whose son Philip was a long-time director of Antofagasta Railways and indeed remained on the board after the company had been acquired by Yugoslav copper tycoon Andronico Luksic. Robert Adeane chaired many of the investment trusts). In 1971, four years after Drayton's death, the group was renamed Drayton Montagu.

Drayton remains an interesting but shadowy figure. The circumstance of his hiring by J. S. Austen, a bachelor Director of 117, who bequeathed his estate to him when he was in his twenties, the absence of official recognition and the real power that he exercised all contribute to the enigma that was Harold Charles

Gilbert Drayton. He had no children and it is not known what happened to his estate, his paintings, his library or to the house itself after he died. There was an oil painting of him by D. Jagger in the possession of British Electric Traction in 1981 at Stratton House, Stratton Street but that too has disappeared. When he died Angus Ogilvy's wife, Princess Alexandra, attended his funeral at Bury St Edmunds; later, his memorial service was held in St Paul's Cathedral. According to Welby it was attended by an enormous concourse.

In 1948 Angus Ogilvy finished his National Service with the Scots Guards and followed his two older brothers into the City. David, the elder, duly inherited the Airlie Earldom but worked for his living for many years at Schroders, before becoming a much-admired Lord Chamberlain in 1984. James, the other brother, became a partner in Rowe & Pitman, a firm of stockbrokers, or rather, other than Cazenove, *the* firm of stockbrokers. Angus, intelligent, handsome and blessed with genuine and natural charm, secured employment with the enigmatic and secretive Harley Drayton, where he prospered. I recall being given a lift by him in the back of his enormous Rolls-Royce from clubland to the City. It had a glass panel to separate the passengers from the chauffeur, and indeed they were quite a common feature in those days. Lord Berners had an upright piano in the back of his Rolls, and the mildly absurd Lord Furness was once abandoned by his chauffeur in Piccadilly in the back of his. Furness had a tendency to hammer on the partition with the silver top of his cane, beseeching the exasperated chauffeur to speed up or slow down. Aware that his employer was unable to drive, the chauffeur, at the end of his tether, stopped the car outside the Ritz in the midst of the traffic, opened the rear door and said 'Drive the ******* thing yourself, my Lord' and disappeared down into Green Park underground station.

Drayton's network of investments was predominantly South and Central American railway companies, but included South African and Rhodesian enterprises. London & Rhodesia Lands was moribund and in 1955 Harley Drayton decided that it needed to be reinvigorated and dispatched Ogilvy to Harare to do something about it. Unknown to Ogilvy at that time, there was living in Rhodesia an unusual man and it remains unclear why he was living there. His name (manufactured like so much of his make-up) was Rowland, although he had been born Fuhrhop. Of German / Indian origin, his parents had settled in England before the war and were promptly interned on the Isle of Man at the outbreak of war, to Rowland's ever-lasting fury, which was further compounded by the death of his mother during her internment.

Rowland had been educated at Churcher's College before embarking on a career which had a touch of Arthur English about it. (English was a comedian well known in the 1940s for portraying spivs.) He had some entrepreneurial participation during the Berlin airlift, at which point he met Freddie Laker whose first aircraft company was born out of the Berlin crisis. Then Rowland mysteriously removed himself to Rhodesia. There, clad in cravat, blazer and suede shoes he began his enduring African entrepreneurial career and, fatally for Ogilvy, their paths crossed when Ogilvy arrived in Salisbury. C. G. Rogers, then Standard Bank Manager, arranged a lunch in his honour to which he invited 'Tiny' Rowland. The details of the lunch are unknown but it is clear that Rowland cast his malign spell over Ogilvy.

By this time Ogilvy had married (1967) Princess Alexandra and accordingly was not only the emissary of a powerful controller of funds but also a member of the Royal Family.

Rowland could scarcely contain himself and came up with a plan. This in effect provided for London & Rhodesia Lands to issue shares to Rowland in exchange for his farming and dealership / agency interests. The immediate result was that Rowland became the owner of 29 per cent of the company, which changed its name to LONRHO. He also became the Chief Executive. Ogilvy initially became a Non-Executive Director but shortly afterwards an Executive Director alongside Alan Ball, the Deputy Chairman, and Fred Butcher, the Finance Director.

There then began a dizzying series of acquisitions, two of which were to be the source of trouble for Angus. The first was a mining company, Coronation Syndicate. Fifty per cent of this was owned by the shareholders and 50 per cent by Rowland, Ball & Ogilvy. This structure was conceived by Rowland and resulted in the Coronation Syndicate shareholders putting up 100 per cent of the costs for developing its copper mine whilst Rowland, Ball & Ogilvy were carried. This was at least a breach of exchange control at the time. It is entirely possible that Ogilvy was unaware of this arrangement but either way it was too late. Rowland had ensnared him in his web. The other issue concerned the Beira Oil Pipeline (owned and operated by LONRHO), which was judged to have breached the sanctions imposed on Rhodesia after Ian Smith's Unilateral Declaration of Independence (UDI).

All this resulted in a Department of Trade enquiry into LONRHO's affairs, which led to a mild censure of Ogilvy. As a result of this censure Ogilvy felt that he should resign from LONRHO (thereby incurring Rowland's wrath) as well as from the fifteen other directorships he held. It was a measure of his competence and intelligence that these included the Midland Bank (probably thanks to the influence of Drayton) and others, two of which to their credit – The Rank Organisation and MEPC – refused to accept his resignation. Sir David Davies, then the young Finance Director of MEPC, recalls the meeting at which he and Jack Hughes, senior partner of Jones, Lang & Wotton, argued that Ogilvy had done no wrong, and they carried the board with them. Shortly afterwards Sotheby's offered him an executive role, which he accepted and at which he excelled. By this time he had jettisoned the Rolls and had become an evangelical cyclist. He was a familiar sight bicycling from St James's Palace to Sotheby's office in New Bond Street.

Throughout his enduringly happy marriage to Princess Alexandra, and despite his heavy work commitments, he acted as a faithful and popular consort. After his resignations he threw himself vigorously into work for charities, many of which had good cause to be grateful to him. It was really at this point that I came to know him well. Unknown to him I was an usher at his wedding: my Battalion of the Grenadier Guards had been stationed at Wellington Barracks at the time, and the young officers were detailed to help with the proceedings at Westminster Abbey. He had long been tortured with back pain and always had a strained appearance as a result. I think I am correct in saying he further suffered through being deficient of a kidney. These problems he compounded by chain smoking – ultimately the source of his demise.

His charitable work was Herculean; impossible to mention the numerous causes he supported. It was through The Prince's Trust that I came to know him and I admired the courteous and patient way he dealt with its affairs. He had an endearing habit of finishing a sentence with an interrogatory 'Are you with me?', to which the answer was often 'Not entirely, Angus.' All of the charities with which he was associated flourished, not least The

Prince's Trust itself, now ably led by one of our leading philanthropists and businessmen, Sir Lloyd Dorfman.

Angus Ogilvy I would definitely characterise as an unacknowledged hero. His behaviour was exemplary: as consort to Princess Alexandra, as a successful businessman, and in the triumph over adversity of health and the malign influence of 'Tiny' Rowland.

12

PROSPECTING IN EAST AFRICA

I HAD A house in Orange Grove Drive in Harare, opposite the Forestry Commission. It was really a bungalow, but it sat well within a five-acre garden with a veranda, a swimming pool and some magnificent trees, to which we added three mahogany trees to mark the births of our three boys. I spent many peaceful hours on that veranda seated in a planters chair with a Gilbert's No 1, the local version of Pimm's, in my hand, gazing out at the garden and listening to various pleasing African sounds, including distant traffic, whilst my wife painted or gardened ebulliently.

There was a gardener, Peter, who worked incessantly. There was also a 'houseboy', Isaac, aged seventy and alas now dead. He had been the valet to Simon Ramsay, 16th Earl of Dalhousie when he was the Governor of Southern Rhodesia and had accordingly been well trained. Dalhousie, who had won the Military Cross serving with the Black Watch in

North Africa, teamed up with two other war heroes, 'Potter' Miller Mundy and Jack Pringle (both of whom had also won MCs), when they retired and returned to London. They secured an office in Albemarle Street – a hundred yards from White's Club – but no one discovered what they really did there! Dalhousie was elected MP for Forfarshire, becoming a Conservative Whip in 1946.

In those days Colonial Governors' wives were attended by several ladies-in-waiting and one of these, Lady Harriot, was very grand and married a similarly cerebral and musical Judge, Mark Tennant.

The bungalow centred around two rooms – the first was the dining room with a large circular table, at which we ate curried prawns and roast chicken virtually every night, and in the morning enormous breakfasts cooked by Isaac. The walls were hung with African paintings assembled by my wife. The other room I converted into a library containing mostly African natural history and historical books, although the mother of our local Managing Director Nicholas Graham, the widow of a Brigadier, ran an excellent second-hand bookshop in nearby Borrowdale from which I managed to acquire a number of Ian Fleming first editions, still in their dust wrappers, for a handful of Zimbabwe dollars.

After breakfast I would sally forth into the centre of Harare where we had an office in a hideous building known as the Karigamombe Centre. I think we were on the twelfth floor and, after once being stuck in the lift for thirty minutes – which seemed like thirty days – I used to labour up the staircase.

We operated four mines: three smallish ones (Royal Family, Mali Green and Peach Tree, managed from our Bulawayo office) and the Freda Rebecca, the country's largest gold mine, producing 100,000 ounces per year. This was located an hour's drive north of Harare in the settlement of Bindura and was ably directed on site by a handsome and genial Dutchman, Max Kraan, who had previously run a large tin mine, Kisenge. I became very fond of Max and his wife and enjoyed many sundowners on the terrace of the mine manager's house. Max liked cocktails but he also chain-smoked a lethal Dutch cheroot known as a Villager, which was eventually his undoing.

I would characterise Max as firm but fair, and he was respected by all, in particular the mine workers who never withdrew their labour whilst Max was in charge. His catchphrase was 'can of worms', which he applied to virtually any entity over which he had no control – the Government and the Ministry of Mines in particular.

We used to drive to Bindura but when it was necessary to visit the other open-cast operations we would fly from Harare to Bulawayo and always stay in the Bulawayo Club. This was, and is, housed in a beautiful colonial building with courtyard and fountain and a piano nobile, which contained an enormous dining room and a library replete with Africana books and many Cecil Rhodes busts, photographs and ephemera. There was also a huge bar and a billiards room. Two elderly members, who had lived in the club for fifty years but had fallen out, sat at opposite ends of this room.

After I married Blondel, who is of Caribbean origin, she joined me on a visit to Bulawayo. The bedrooms were spartan to say the least, but entirely adequate. The practice was for one of the African waiters, dressed in a white sari and scarlet sashes, to bring guests a cup of tea at 7 a.m. The first morning Blondel stayed there the waiter duly knocked and entered what he expected to be a white male's bedroom. Not only was my wife in the bed, but she was *not white*, which prompted him to drop the entire tray on the hardwood floor – never had he seen a woman, let alone a black one, in a bedroom before!

On another occasion our Deputy Chairman, Tommy Pilkington, and I were staying at the club, along with Colin Campbell who was then *The Times* mining correspondent. When not in his office Colin lived on the racecourse and was most intimidated by Tommy, who was the Senior Steward of the Jockey Club. On one evening Tommy and I hosted a dinner at the club to enable Colin to meet our management team. This was a fairly fraught time in Zimbabwe and the white community had nothing complimentary to say about the Government. It would not be inaccurate or unfair to name our three senior executives, Roy Pitchford, Richard Armitage and Max Kraan, as well-fed. Colin, Tommy and I on the other hand were very much on the attenuated side. We sat down to dinner and I winced every time one of my executives repeatedly said, 'The country is going to the dogs,' or 'a can of worms', accompanied by an order to the bewildered waiter for 'More wine please, and another fillet steak.' I never knew what impression this had on the chain-smoking Colin, who probably weighed all of eight stone. I do, however, remember the evening concluding happily with two games of snooker.

Soon after I received a letter from a Mr C. A. Rudd, who was the Chairman of the Bulawayo Club, asking me whether I would speak to the club and explain what the company was doing in Zimbabwe. So I agreed to this and asked Rudd for a drink before my speech. It quickly became apparent that he did not wish to hear any ringing endorsements from me about the future of mining in the country and gave me a sour introduction, followed by some sarcastic questions. I was pretty angry because I had made a special trip to Bulawayo for the purpose of raising people's spirits. To be met with such negativism was depressing. It was at least one in the eye for him that shortly afterwards we opened our first open-cast mine in Africa at Filabusi, near Bulawayo.

It was at this time that I mistakenly conceived the idea of acquiring a company called Aberfoyle, listed in London but with its assets in Zimbabwe. It was a so-called conglomerate, owning an engineering business, a textile company and an enormous sugar estate. The shrewd Tommy, my wife and I visited all these subsidiaries and were of the view, which I reluctantly endorsed, that this was not one of my better concepts. I expect it all ended up in the hands of some smooth Indian, although the sugar estate was acquired by Anglo American's sugar arm Tongaat Hulett, which involved us in dealing with David Gass, a most agreeable South African. Alas Mugabe frustrated that acquisition, which would, with Tongaat's experience, have earned Zimbabwe substantial foreign exchange earnings as well as employment for the local Africans.

At the time we were beginning to make significant profits from our Zimbabwe mines and we resolved to reduce our Zimbabwe exposure and examine other pan-African opportunities. Eventually we had an operating mine in Ghana, Ayanfuri, an extremely successful project funded jointly by the excellent Lebanese businessman Albert Abela's organisations and with project finance provided by Barclays Bank. The next country on our list was Tanzania and, guided by our wise exploration manager Peter Cowley, we successfully bid for the Geita gold project on Lake Victoria – a brilliant concept.

Tommy and I, together with the Managing Director of our Australian company, Walter Penninger, set off for Dar es Salaam to commence negotiations with Colonel Kikwete, then Minister of Mines and subsequently Tanzania's President. We stayed at the Kilimanjaro Hotel, deficient in any form of comfort such as air conditioning or hot water, but which boasted an excellent restaurant on the roof. Being marooned there for a weekend we elected to make a day trip to Zanzibar, and Tommy and I, incorrigible clubmen, tracked down the Zanzibar Club. To say that it was a shadow of its former self would be an understatement. It was effectively a ruin – rebels had even unleashed their fury on the snooker table which incredibly they had smashed into a thousand pieces, all of which were piled up in a corner. Despite this we had a memorable lunch of lobster. On our way out I noticed a door with 'Library' inscribed on it. Although locked I prevailed upon the waiter to open the door, which revealed a treasure trove of African titles, all of which had escaped the depredation of the rebels. I often wonder what eventually happed to it – happily the club is now a successful hotel.

A charity, The Remembrance Trust, which I chair, is currently engaged in repairing the pre-1914 graves in the Naval cemetery in Zanzibar, mostly of British sailors killed on the anti-slavery operations in the late nineteenth century.

Eventually, Colonel Kikwete awarded us the Geita Concession in the face of fierce competition from much larger organisations. It quickly became apparent that Peter Cowley's confidence was well placed, but we became the victims of our own success. Our foresight led to our nemesis, in the form of an inevitable bid for the company from Ashanti Goldfields, as it was evident that Geita was going to be a major gold producer. Indeed, the deposit turned out to be the largest gold discovery on the African continent since the last war.

13

GOLD MINING IN
WEST AFRICA

LUFF RESOURCES ACCORDINGLY now
existed only as a subsidiary of Ashanti,
and I determined to start all over
again, forming Cluff Minerals which owned,
other than various platinum prospects in South
Africa, a gold deposit in Burkina Faso known as
Kalsaka, located about three hours' drive from
Ouagadougou. The South African platinum
interests were obtained by a Terence Watkinson,
for whom I had no respect, and I resolved to
form another company leaving Watkinson, the
sponsor of the platinum interests, to attempt
to develop them whilst I vested Kalsaka in a
new company and regained my independence.
Douglas Chikohora, a Zimbabwean geologist
who had been much involved in the discovery and development of the Ayanfuri mine in
Ghana, joined me and our primary task became
the development of Kalsaka. We also acquired
from BRGM, a French state-funded mining

organisation, a deposit in the Ivory Coast, which caused us much anguish, though now it is evolving into a world-class gold mine.

We also became aware of a gold discovery at Baomahun in Sierra Leone, which oddly belonged to a company owned by an old New York friend of mine, Ronald Winston. Ronald, one of two sons of the legendary Harry Winston of diamond fame, is a chemist by training and he lived an adventurous life as diamond purchaser for Savimbi in Angola and as proprietor and Chairman of Harry Winston, until its sale about fifteen years ago. Ronald is a clever man and possessed of a kind heart as well as a keen sense of humour.

The Kalsaka Mine is now mined out, having produced about 60,000 ounces a year for seven years. It was an open-cast operation and ultimately profitable, although because of its low grade it proved difficult to finance. This put us under some pressure from the Minister of Mines to get a move on, and we wound up having an opening ceremony despite the fact that the mine was not ready to start production. When we finally did start the workers inadvertently put a sacred stone into the crushing machine, which nearly resulted in a riot. I seem to recall that we were almost permanently endeavouring to head off all manner of stoppages.

The situation was not improved when, as often happens, I was approached by well-meaning parents seeking a job for their child. On this occasion such an approach resulted in us hiring an attractive young girl with aristocratic credentials and possessing a degree in geology. It so happened that we were short of a geologist at Kalsaka and I offered her a job there, coupled with a warning that it was a tough assignment in spartan conditions. She jumped at the chance and was duly employed and based at the Kalsaka Mine. Shortly afterwards there was another labour stoppage and, leading the angry workers, bearing a sign reading 'Filthy British, Go Home', was none other than our feisty aristocratic beauty from Bristol University. No good turn goes unpunished, as someone accurately said.

I must have been to the Kalsaka Mine on dozens of occasions. However, in forty years of trips I don't recall driving myself anywhere – one always seemed to have a 'driver'. Even the Minister of Mines drove me back from the mine to Ouagadougou on one occasion, when I recall enquiring why there seemed to be no French Colonial buildings anywhere: 'We blew them up' he said succinctly.

It was on this trip that I was informed that the President, Blaise Compaoré, wished to invest me as a Chevalier of the Country's Order of Chivalry. I was much bucked by this acknowledgement of the work that we had all contributed to Kalsaka, although I nearly passed out at the investiture, held in the open air and involving sitting with no shade for three hours in temperatures above 40 degrees.

My final visit to Ouagadougou happened to coincide with the eruption of the Icelandic volcano Eyjafjallajökull, which grounded most of the world's airline system, at least in the northern hemisphere. My three-day visit was extended to ten days before I could exit from Burkina, which I finally did by military aircraft to Accra and from Accra (where I celebrated my seventieth birthday, not the grand party planned in London) to Dubai, from Dubai to Paris, and from Paris by car to Calais where I crossed the Channel as a foot passenger. It is worth reflecting that the volcano that erupted then is the smaller of two. The larger one last erupted in 1789 and caused the failure of the crops in France, which was given as one reason for the French Revolution. The larger is issuing sinister signs of erupting again.

Meanwhile I was conducting a prolonged

negotiation with Ronald Winston regarding his Sierra Leone gold deposit. Apparently his father, on his deathbed, had urged Ronald not to relinquish this licence, as a renowned professor of geology at Columbia University had advised him that it had the makings of a major gold mine. We eventually issued Cluff shares for the unlisted Winston Mines, whose sole asset was the Baomahun gold deposit.

I then set off for my first visit to Sierra Leone. The airport is some three hours' drive from the centre of Freetown, but this travelling time can be greatly reduced by chartering a boat from the airport beach. This process involved being carried on the shoulders of a huge fisherman, then dumped into a smaller boat, transferred to a large boat which motors erratically for an hour before the process is reversed and the passenger eventually staggers ashore in the capital, covered in sardines and saltwater.

The Baomahun deposit required a further eight-hour drive from Freetown into the jungle, where previously adits had been driven into a range of hills – now the home of bats and rats and theoretically of a commercial gold mine.

How best to determine the scale of the deposit and then how to develop it caused much discussion and argument, and it all came at the cost of much money. Were we to seek to produce 40,000 ounces per annum from a 'cheap and cheerful' open-pit operation at a development cost of $10 million, or, as the technical staff preferred, aim to produce 200,000 ounces at a cost of $200 million? (So far, twenty years later, neither of these scenarios has eventuated.) Then suddenly an Englishman, previously happily unknown to me, materialised, claiming to have special status with the arrogant and obnoxious Minister of Mines. The details of this approach remain sub judice as I have given evidence to the authorities regarding this behaviour. There are no commercial considerations at stake as the Baomahun deposit now belongs to another unconnected party. However, it did highlight the seamier side of African business.

This episode rather overshadowed my decision to withdraw from Africa and return to the North Sea, where my commercial career had begun in 1970 (as reported in my first book, *Get On With It*, 2016). I had become increasingly concerned that, notwithstanding the improvement in the education of politicians and bureaucrats, it was becoming increasingly difficult to compete with companies that had no regard for the law, and were happy to corrupt officials in order to obtain their objectives.

Many of these companies are of Chinese, Indian or Russian origin, whose appreciation of corporate governance is slight to non-existent. Others were owned by people who knew precisely that what they were doing was wrong, but who had constructed labyrinthine corporate structures, in many cases in so-called 'havens' such as the British Virgin Islands and the Cayman Islands, where they secured complete anonymity from the law and the taxman. These were, and are, havens for the bad not the good.

Many were the times when I ruefully reflected that the maligned colonial system had been replaced by a form of independence that conferred less benefit on the African population than had obtained previously, while providing venal politicians and officials with uncontrolled opportunity for personal benefit and aggrandisement.

To an extent the Commonwealth had acted as a discipline for its members until Tony Blair, the villain of so many pieces, in his evangelical pro-European drive, judged the Commonwealth to be outmoded, patronising and 'not modern'.

14

THE AGM

THE AGM is a curiously unsatisfactory although unavoidable event. I must have chaired well over a hundred of them during my commercial career, and although some had their difficulties, I have never had to deal with a request for a vote on a motion. I always accorded AGMs great importance and treated the shareholders with courtesy and deference. Only a fool would do otherwise. Alas, there are quite a number of foolish chairmen.

I learned my first lesson about forty years ago whilst chairing a meeting of Cluff Oil at Brown's Hotel. I had taken my wristwatch off in order to monitor the length of my speech. When I closed the meeting I moved to recover the watch, only to find it had disappeared – presumably a shareholder had helped himself in lieu of a dividend!

We held some of our AGMs at the Royal Automobile Club, where one year I noticed an elderly man in the front row with a hearing aid, which was emitting crackling noises. When the time came for questions he struggled to his feet.

'Mr Chairman' he quavered, 'I would like to congratulate you and your colleagues on a magnificent job...' He then paused as we preened ourselves ... 'Unfortunately *I can't*' he rasped, and then unveiled a serious of longwinded and deranged questions.

The following year he was back again; however, before he could get to his feet an enormous African gentleman of menacing aspect took the floor and said how grateful Africans should be for all we had done operating mines in Zimbabwe and Ghana and giving employment to so many people. Applause from the assembled company and silence from our tormentor. The following year he was absent and hopefully had gone to the great AGM in the sky.

Too many companies seem to regard the AGM as a tiresome chore and are wary of, rather than welcoming to, shareholders. Even more unfortunate is the patronising attitude adopted in some circumstances. For example, my mother was persuaded to become a member of Lloyd's of London, having been beguiled by some slippery sophist with promises of a cornucopia of benefits. Admittedly, a compelling reason for joining Lloyd's at the time was the 90 per cent tax on 'unearned' income. Any income that the member received was judged to be 'earned', and accordingly taxed at a lower rate. Unfortunately, through a combination of incompetence and dishonesty, there was no income at any rate – only losses. Once a year, before the Lloyd's implosion, my mother was summoned to a lunch at the Savoy where she was given the impression that she and the other 'names' in her syndicate were fortunate to have the opportunity of fraternising with such swells. Alas, they were crooks not swells, and did immediate and catastrophic damage to those that trusted them and lasting damage to the reputation of Lime Street.

I became suspicious at the fast rate those Lloyd's agents lived – jetting off every week to Deauville and Monte Carlo. A friend of mine told me that he had once chartered a yacht from the man who managed his syndicate. He was chatting to the Captain on the bridge one morning and observed to him what a beautiful yacht it was.

'You should see the other one,' the Captain responded.

I knew at the time a clever but controversial Lloyd's professional, Christopher Moran. He had no formal education but was possessed of a good brain and a ruthless commercial ethos. He had joined Lloyd's as a lowly clerk and quickly realised that after lunch the gin-sodden members became rather somnolent. He therefore resolved to start his own broking firm, which opened for business only from 2.30 in the afternoon. Having devised a new form of aviation insurance he quickly prospered and made himself and his 'names' a lot of money. The irony was that he was eventually expelled by a Star Chamber process so shocking that the leading solicitor of the time agreed to advise him for no fee. He subsequently proved to be a useful member of the charity community, particularly in a medical and musical context.

15

Lord Rathcavan

AN APOCRYPHAL TALE: one evening in the 1970s, a car driven by an Irishman south from Bordeaux to Biarritz collided with a wild boar heading east across the famously straight road that bisects large pine forests for a hundred miles or so. The boar was dead on impact and the car a wreck, as was our hero who lay moaning and unable to move. Car after car roared past, too intent on their destination to permit any act of mercy by intervening. At last a car stopped and four Frenchmen got out. Thank heavens, deliverance at last, sighed our hero. The Frenchmen picked up the dead boar, placed it in the boot of their car and sped off. Despair overwhelmed our hero, until an hour later another car stopped, out of which there stepped an Englishman.

'Are you all right, old boy?'

'No, I am not. I am dying and I must get to hospital.'

'Fred', the Englishman, duly conveyed his

wounded charge to a hospital near Bordeaux. Our hero, now Lord Rathcavan but then the Hon. Hugh O'Neill, lived on, although his legs were severely damaged. He was naturally grateful to Fred, although it has to be said that the gratitude rapidly subsided with the frequency of phone calls from his saviour, which had a certain maddening consistency.

'Hello Hugh, it's Fred. You remember I saved your life? I am a bit short at the moment. You couldn't send me another £500? Thanks squire.'

This is an interesting parable of the French and the English.

Hugh O'Neill served as an officer in the Irish Guards before becoming a financial journalist with *The Irish Times* and *The Financial Times*, and in 1982 I asked him to join the board of *The Spectator*. He is a clever man, possessed of a caustic wit complemented by a singular charm.

He has been a dedicated champion of the Northern Irish cause and has served the community in a number of respects, including a period as Chairman of the Northern Ireland Airports. One evening he took the last flight back to Belfast from Heathrow and had no doubt treated himself to a couple of scotches on the plane. He had intended, when he disembarked, to collect his car from the airport carpark and drive it home. However, to his dismay he found he had mislaid his keys. Accordingly he approached a policeman and explained his predicament, adding for effect that, as the policeman doubtless was aware, he was Mr O'Neill, the Chairman of the Airport. The next thing he knew was that he was sitting in the back of a police van being cautioned for impersonating the Chairman of Belfast Airport whilst under the influence of alcohol!

His real talent lay in the catering business and he founded a restaurant in the Brompton Road that became legendary. He also served on the management board of the Savoy Hotel. After succeeding his father as Lord Rathcavan in 1994 he became a diligent member of the House of Lords.

Of all my contemporaries he was the most consistently good company, although challenged by ill health, probably originating with that Bordeaux boar incident. He was also a great friend of Geoffrey Keating (see Kim Philby, Chapter 19).

16

CONRAD BLACK

IT IS RECORDED in Tom Bower's book about Conrad Black, *Dancing On The Edge,* that such was the chaos prevailing when Lord Hartwell made his first and only visit to America (to save the *Telegraph* newspaper group) that he thought he was meeting Conrad Ritblat, not Conrad Black. He went on the Concorde and returned the same day! That is one of the few benign sentences in the book. Tom is the master of this particular genre, but *Dancing On The Edge* boils down to the case for the prosecution. I knew Conrad well and feel that I should present another side of him, which indeed I did when I wrote to the Chicago Judge Amy J. St. Eve on his behalf. I should also record that I am a longstanding friend of Daniel Colson, Conrad's right-hand man. Dan had been a partner of leading Canadian lawyers Stikeman Elliott, and had worked in their Hong Kong and London offices. As is well known he effectively replaced Andrew Knight as Chief

Executive of *The Telegraph* on his resignation, following his controversial decision to join the Murdoch camp.

After Hollinger bought *The Spectator* I saw a lot of Dan. He exhibited complete loyalty to his ex-university comrade Conrad, whilst being refreshingly unimpressed by journalists. With his grasp of commercial imperatives, his legal training and his complete absence of ego he remains both a formidable and attractive individual. His probity has never been in question. Accordingly, his assertion that Conrad never stole a cent carries the authority of a lawyer who was at the centre of Black's affairs throughout the *Telegraph* saga. Black has been sentenced (a significantly lower one, incidentally, than many of his tormentors had hoped) and I do not propose to challenge that other than to aver that greed is not a crime, nor is arrogance.

There is no doubt that hubris and a strange naïveté were the catalysts of his demise. His downfall was precipitated by his high-handed treatment of the respected fund manager Tweedy, Browne during a Hollinger AGM, at which Tweedy, Browne had sought to enquire into Conrad's expenses; instead of answering sensibly Conrad gave the impression that it was none of their business! Alas, humility is the handmaiden of really admirable people and in this instance it was lacking, although the Non-Executive Directors should share the blame as one of their important responsibilities to the shareholders is to identify any signs of the CEO developing an ego. As is so often the case they were mesmerised by a tycoon whose ego had overtaken his judgement. In Conrad Black's case his choice of Barbara Amiel as his second wife injected a further toxic element into the Hollinger cocktail.

However, my purpose here is to record a more benign and useful side to Conrad Black's newspaper proprietorship, and to pay tribute to a really rather remarkable character. Conrad is definitely not a morning or even afternoon man. During Hollinger's proprietorship of *The Spectator* magazine, which I chaired, Conrad was appointed as a Non-Executive, as was Dan Colson, along with the existing board comprising Christopher Fildes, Sir Patrick Sheehy, Lord (John) King, Norman Tebbit and Kimberley Fortier.

These board meetings were curious affairs, although they certainly represented an important discipline for the Editor and the Publisher, both of whom were required to sing for their supper. We met at my office in St James's at

6.30 p.m. and afterwards adjourned for dinner in the Cavendish Room at Brooks's Club at 8 p.m. This would be Conrad's first meeting of the day; nonetheless Conrad always arrived an hour late for everything. As he entered the room he raised his right hand in a papal salute. He was always dignified in dress and ever courteous to his colleagues. My difficulty was to start the meeting at 6.30 and conclude it with time to greet our guests at Brooks's by 8. Despite having a minor nervous breakdown keeping it all going without knowing when, if at all, Conrad would show up, I do have a happy recollection of them. Conrad's contributions to the meetings were always succinct, as indeed were those of Barbara, by this time also a Non-Executive.

Dinner – and a few glasses of wine – always rendered Conrad a most genial companion with his dry aperçus matched by his truly astonishing reservoir of knowledge.

Dan Colson maintained that Conrad practically never put in an appearance at *The Telegraph* office in Canary Wharf. What he did all day until launching himself from Hampstead to the West End I know not, although I expect he was constantly adding to that reservoir of knowledge in his library. Latterly he moved to a rather dotty but more appropriate house in Cottesmore Gardens, where I attended various parties, although Barbara treated me with marked reserve, despite, or perhaps because of, the fact that she had known me before either of us was married.

I would occasionally go to Canary Wharf myself to lunch with Dan Colson a deux, where we would have a laugh about life and how exasperating certain journalists could be (Frank Johnson in particular). I remember remarking how civil Conrad always was, rather to my surprise, and how unconfrontational he was inclined to be. He had just asked me if I could have a word with one of *The Spectator* contributors whose tendency to pin the more attractive staff members to the wall was causing consternation. Dan confirmed that anything involving firing was his task alone, reminding me of Henry Keswick's description of Martin Lampard, Senior Partner of Ashursts, as 'an expert sacking lawyer'!

When Conrad's world collapsed, and he served a six-year prison sentence, he took it on the chin and there was no sign of self-pity as his erstwhile friends took to the hills. I, at any rate, recall him with affection as a benevolent proprietor and a man of courage and intellectual consequence. It is incredible to reflect that during his days as proprietor *The Telegraph* had an average audited circulation of around 1.2 million copies per day. Now the equivalent sales are below 400,000.

The *Spectator* editors during the Black proprietorship were all distinguished journalists: Charles Moore, Dominic Lawson, Frank Johnson and Boris Johnson. The latter told me recently that he will always be grateful to me for preventing a board endeavour to cut his salary!

17

Hong Kong

I AM WRITING this in Hong Kong in a wonderful house at Shek O overlooking the South China Sea. Although this is my first visit to Hong Kong in ten years, I did come frequently between 1980 and 1995 whilst we were active in the search for hydrocarbons in the South China and Yellow Seas. The frequency of my trips and the friendships which evolved gave me an interest in Hong Kong's history, and more particularly in the implications for its future as seen at the time. The abiding theme which ran through most conversations with the intelligent members of the Chinese community was an indignation that they were not being consulted by the Colonial Government about what was, after all, their future. Thanks in part to the wisdom of the Governors of Hong Kong in the 1960s, 70s and 80s – notably Messrs Grantham, Black, MacLehose, Youde and Wilson – complemented by the outstanding calibre of the so-called Financial Secretaries Messrs

Cowperthwaite, Haddon-Cave and Bremridge
– the Hong Kong Government adopted a very
light touch and kept Government off the people's back (an income tax return occupied no
more than half of an A4 page). The result was
sustained growth from the end of the Second
World War, right through to the 1997 handover.

The other heroes in this cavalcade were
the bankers, particularly the Chairman of the
Hong Kong & Shanghai Bank during and after
the war, Sir Arthur Morse. He took a robust
approach to providing credit to the trading,
property and shipping companies. His courage
was endorsed and continued by most of his
successors, two of whom, Jake Saunders and
Michael Sandberg (the latter very much an
investment banker), I knew well.

Jake Saunders was a tall, cheerful individual
with an impatient streak. He had fought with
distinction in the war (as many others also did)
winning the DSO and the MC for conspicu-
ous and repeated gallantry in the East Surrey
Regiment. It was he who quickly recognised
the potential for growth in the shipping business, and the legendary Chinese tycoon, Sir Y.
K. Pao, became a favoured client. Now that
Jardine Matheson has a market capitalisation
of $45 billion it is hard to imagine that in the

early sixties Jardines (and Swires) had capitalisation in the mere tens of millions of pounds. The wisdom and enterprise of the Swire and Keswick families created the massive companies of today, which retain their dynastic bias. The shareholders can wish for nothing else. The Swires (Liverpool English), the Keswicks (Lowland Scots) were joined by the Kadoories (Iranian Jewish) who founded China Light and Power, Hong Kong's foremost utility company. Hutchison Whampoa was rather colourfully run by another war hero, Sir Douglas Clague, POW escapee and racehorse breeder, whose high-risk speculations and financial mismanagement ran Hutchinson Whampoa into the ground. It was delivered by the Hong Kong Bank into the control of a Chinese client, Li Ka-Shing, who must now run one of the most successful property and trading empires in the world. Hutchison incidentally was run for a critical period by the estimable Englishman Simon Murray, another colourful figure.

In the so-called 'run up' to 1997 I had cause to spend much of my time in Beijing and Hong Kong. I had first visited Beijing in 1980, only thirty-nine years ago, since when the velocity of change has been staggering. Ironically it was Chairman Mao – the Great Helmsman – who argued that when change came it had to be 'absolute' change. So everything was reduced to its lowest common denominator – and libraries and universities destroyed. Mao felt that China (where indeed examinations to enter the civil service were unchanged for two thousand years until the 1930s) had become sclerotic. He was right, but could not have imagined that within fifty years of his death his successors would have caused another cultural revolution, but this time liberating the Chinese people's thirst for enterprise.

Hong Kong of course had reverted to Chinese rule during this second revolution. It may be that this was inevitable, but it seemed to me during those ten years prior to 1997 that the situation could have had a quite different outcome. There was virtually no consultation with the Hong Kong Chinese about their destiny and since many of them had escaped from totalitarian China to Hong Kong they did not relish the prospect of the handover. Could there have been a different solution? After all, China was chronically short of foreign exchange at the time. Possibly the Hong Kong Chinese could have come up with a formula to extend the UK's lease for a further fifty years, accompanied by a substantial annual rental payment. In the event, Chinese conduct of Hong Kong's affairs has largely preserved the integrity and prosperity of the territory.

A shame then that 'Chris' Patten's appointment as the final Governor of Hong Kong led to a deterioration in relations between our two countries. I have no personal animus regarding Patten, indeed he was always very courteous to me on the few occasions I met him in Hong Kong, which included lunching with him and David Tang on the day of my wedding in St Stephen's Chapel in Stanley. (My wife and I donated a stained-glass window in honour of our marriage and in tribute to those nurses and soldiers killed by the Japanese in 1941, and to those who died in Stanley camp before its liberation by Admiral Harcourt in 1945.) However, I always thought there was much that was self-serving about his period as Governor. Instead of having the elementary courtesy of paying his respects to the Chinese Government before taking up his post he instead lectured them about democracy and got on their nerves without having anything to show for it. Had he gone to Beijing and introduced himself as a living casualty of democracy (having lost his seat in Bath at the 1992 election) and stated that he was minded to see more democracy in Hong Kong before the end of British rule I have no doubt they would have listened and co-operated. The fact that the Chinese delegation turned their backs as the Royal Yacht steamed out of Hong Kong, bearing him and Prince Charles away after the handover ceremony, is indeed sad.

18

Big Bang

I HAVE IN front of me the list of members of the Stock Exchange in 1973. There were over three hundred firms, a few in Liverpool, Manchester, Newcastle, Birmingham, Edinburgh and Glasgow, but with the vast majority in London, EC2 or EC3. The names include firms famous at the time: Akroyd & Smithers, Buckmaster & Moore, James Capel, WI Carr, De Zoete & Bevan, Kitcat & Aitken, Laing & Cruikshank, Messels, Pember & Boyle, Rowe & Pitman, Scrimgeour & Zorn, Leigh-Hunt, Vickers da Costa. The names of the Partners are themselves nostalgic, exuding upper-class backgrounds: Viscount Savernake, Hon J. F. Yarde-Buller, J. R. Henderson, P. B. Mitford-Slade, Sir Charles Frederick, Sir Martin Wilkinson, J. H. Bevan, the Marquess of Tavistock, Viscount Chandos, O. P. Dawnay, Hon. D. C. Chichester, W. A. Bromley-Davenport, H. A. Hely-Hutchinson, P. R. Meinertzhagen, Lord Roger Manners,

Sir Edward Lewis, Erland D'Abo, Sir David Hill-Wood, Lord Glendyne, Ralph Vickers and Julian Martin Smith ... about two thousand of them. Many of these, grand or not, boasted wartime decorations, particularly the Distinguished Service Order and the Military Cross.

The stockbroker pre-1984 was often ill versed in corporate matters and existed on a mixture of charm and persuasion. An example of this species, of whom there were many, was Dickie Birch-Reynardson, a partner in the firm of Myers & Co., of whom the senior partner was a grand City figure, Erland D'Arbo. Dickie had been a Major in the Grenadier Guards, had a scented moustache, a carnation in his lapel and always a double-breasted waistcoat with a gold watch chain covering his ample stomach. During the rigid Exchange Control years, in which you had to declare any currency over the £50 allowance when leaving the UK, a friend of mine found himself behind Dickie at Heathrow Airport. Dickie was proceeding past the customs officer when he was stopped and asked to open his briefcase. Having turned ashen white he did so, to reveal £5,000 in new bank notes.

'That stupid secretary of mine has packed

the wrong briefcase,' he expostulated, at which point he was asked to go behind a screen.

Shortly afterwards he was seen to resume his progress, with a slightly lighter briefcase, having no doubt applied his charm to the customs officer who may well, as so often the case in those days, have also been in the Grenadier Guards.

One of those broking firms was known as Quilter, Goodison, and I recall lunching there in 1978 with the senior partner, Nicholas Goodison. A cerebral, civil and quiet man, it was he who became the catalyst for the drastic change in the architecture of the City known as Big Bang – so drastic a change that virtually none of those three hundred firms active in 1973 existed at all by 1983. How did this happen? And was it necessary?

The two catalysts for change were the lack of capital available to the stockbroking firms themselves and the lack of capital owned by the Partners, who had been unable to save anything during the predominately socialist post-war Governments.

When Mrs Thatcher became Prime Minister she immediately set in train a series of measures that transformed the country and particularly the City. The abolition of Exchange Control came first, liberating the City from domestic-driven financing to the resumption of its previously prominent role as the source of international trade.

In her second administration, as John Plender and Paul Wallace have described in *The Square Mile* (1985), Mrs Thatcher took aim at the 'Club' concept of the City, to which she was temperamentally opposed. So it was that Cecil Parkinson, her Secretary of State for Trade and Industry, and Sir Nicholas Goodison, Chairman of the London Stock Exchange, co-operated to end fixed commission for broking houses.

Cecil Parkinson was a man cast very much in the Thatcher mould, in that he was a North-Country grammar-school boy who gained a scholarship to read English at Cambridge and won a running Blue in the 1950s. He was a thoroughly decent and unstuffy politician, despite the scandal attached to his private life, and steered the City into unchartered waters, ably supported by Sir Nicholas Goodison. Sir Nicholas, who had also studied at King's, Cambridge, had many other interests. He was the Chairman of both the Courtauld Institute and National Art Collection Fund, now the Art Fund, and memorably appeared on *Desert Island Discs* in 1987. Their coalition, with regards to the City brokers, led to the abolition of the jobbing system and to a rush of acquisitions of London broking firms by American financial institutions. Jobbers had created market liquidity by matching buy and sell orders with brokers, but they were not allowed to deal directly with the public.

Before and immediately after the Second World War American business had shunned London in favour of Paris, despite the sclerotic telephone system of the French capital and the language barrier. The combination of Thatcher's reforms, the light touch adopted by the Bank of England, the City's geographic position and the fact that the lingua franca of most markets was English, resulted in a veritable boom for the City, which only ten years before had been reeling from a secondary banking property-lending crisis.

The discovery of North Sea oil further rendered the country a centre of an entirely new industry for the UK, of which the City of London took full advantage. It is now long forgotten that the reforms that gained the epithet Big Bang swept away the traditional City and led to American acquisitions of virtually all the leading British broking and investment banking firms. It also, however, spawned a new generation of smaller, yet more nimble, merchant banking houses that flourish today. Canary Wharf is an eloquent – if not elegant – testimony to the efficiency of Big Bang.

Both Cecil Parkinson and Sir Nicholas Goodison should be more celebrated for their wisdom and dispatch in creating what is now a more dynamic and classless City.

19

KIM PHILBY AND
SIR ROBERT MACKENZIE

I HAVE WRITTEN about Geoffrey Keating before – an amazing individual – but some photographs have come to light since which are of historic significance. Geoffrey was the most famous Second World War photographer, fighting and snapping images of the Norway Campaign, the retreat to Dunkirk, of Monty in the Eighth Army (where he was awarded the Military Cross for valour whilst unarmed, or rather armed only with a camera) and then on to Sicily and Italy. He featured in the photograph of Monty accepting the German surrender at Lüneberg Heath in 1945. Full circle.

One of the first photographs he took is featured in this book. It was of the Army Film and Photographic Unit, together with sundry distinguished journalists and military intelligence figures, and was taken at Christmas 1939 at Arras at the GHQ of the British Expeditionary Force. What is interesting about this photograph is that in the back row, seventh from the left, stands the arch-traitor Kim Philby, then *The Times* correspondent, and also in the same row, fourth from the left, is Sir Robert Mackenzie, Baronet, in Army Intelligence. In 1948 both he and Philby were employed at the British Embassy in Washington where Mackenzie, amazingly, was in charge of security! On the back of the print Geoffrey wrote in 1975: '*The night they met*' with arrows connecting Mackenzie and Philby. The innuendo is clear.

After the war Geoffrey did not find socialist Britain at all to his taste, and secured employment with the Iraq Petroleum Company and then with BP (which he irreverently termed 'British Pederasts') in the Middle East. He was based for most of the time in Iran and served his employers loyally and diligently. He learnt to speak Persian, but the revolution put paid to that world and he returned to London where he set up camp in Three Kings' Yard, opposite Claridge's. This became a West End outpost for BP. However, Sir Maurice Bridgeman, the BP Chairman at the time, found Geoffrey too mettlesome and impossible to control. Legend has it that the last straw occurred when one Saturday morning Sir Maurice made a surprise visit to his office to discover Geoffrey sitting at his desk. For years after he left BP Geoffrey continued his correspondence on the Chairman of BP's office writing paper, c/o Three Kings' Yard SW1.

He then went into business as a property developer with his able friend John Donovan, to their mutual benefit, and was very happily married to Suzie and sired a beautiful daughter Rima.

I often heard Geoffrey refer to Mackenzie as a prime traitor suspect, although the intelligence histories have yet to pick up on it.

By The Way...

I AM WRITING this on a sunny February day in my study overlooking the English Channel. This is where I have lived for fifty years and where I am totally content. Having soldiered and conducted business in the Far East and throughout Africa for most of my life I am now discovering Europe, but also excavating unread volumes in my library. It is my contention that the best library is one which constantly surprises its proprietor. When a guest says:

'You can't have read all these, surely?'

I reply that, happily, I have not, and that is the mark of a good library.

Retirement for me has really been a continuation of my writing and a transition to other activities – in particular my vineyard and a new charity, The Remembrance Trust. However, I spend much of my time reading – not the classics but almost exclusively crime novels written during the Golden Age of the genre in the 1920s to 1950s. It is extraordinary how many intelligent crime novels were published during these years, many of them by academics using pseudonyms. My personal favourite is Freeman Wills Crofts, an Ulsterman whose plots are incomparable, although his characters, including Chief Inspector French, are rather wooden. John Rhode (pseudonym for John Street, an MI5 officer) and Cyril Hare (a Judge) I also rate highly. Part of their charm is that they write of a world now vanished, which they vividly describe and through which I lived. A simpler world where people by and large were content with their lot, and where expectations had not been raised by the internet. Although these books deal with murder there is something refreshingly innocent about them. I fear the internet has rendered innocence an impossible condition in which to exist nowadays.

P. G. Wodehouse similarly wrote about a life which did indeed obtain from Edwardian times to the start of the Second World War, and to read his novels (in my case to re-read them constantly) is like having a bath – you feel cleaner and happier.

Whilst my wife continues to forge a distinguished and useful path in life, I am enjoying the company of our three sons. As the honorary president of the 'Geriatric Fathers Club' it is the primary pleasure and compensation of my advanced age to have the friendship of three boys aged twenty-five, twenty-two and seventeen, ranging in height from 6' 3" (the eldest) to 6' 7" (the youngest). They are all full of promise and I enjoy their irreverent and cheerful presence.

The charity, The Remembrance Trust, I set up with my good friends Richard Kellaway, Brigadier Matt Maer and Hubert Picarda, together with my wife. The impetus derives from the lack of national attention given to the graves and memorials of our fallen soldiers and sailors who died before 1914. The admirable work of the Commonwealth War Graves Commission covers monuments and graves from the First World War to the present. As no one has responsibility for the graves of those killed before 1914, we are striving to play our part in correcting this anomaly.

Since alcohol is in my blood, being descended from three generations of wine shippers, it is no surprise that I have planted a new vineyard behind our house. This will evolve, I hope, into White Cliffs Sparking Wine, and I fully intend playing my part as a consumer as well as producer when the first vintage becomes available in three years' time.

As I can't stand people who are pleased with themselves, I am anxious not to display any element of complacency when describing my life. I have seen too many reversals of fortune, be they of wealth or health, to think otherwise and I remain constantly on guard against the next challenge. So, surrounded by wine, books, my wife and three young sons, I seek, in addition to staying alive, new challenges.

Index

Dorfman, Sir Lloyd 74
Drayton, Harley 65-69, 72
Drayton Montagu 67
Dugdale, Rose 48

Electrolux 49
Enterprise Oil 5
Ecologist Magazine 42
Economist, The 51
English, Arthur 70
Eton 40, 42, 67
Evening Standard 42
Eyjafjallajökull volcano 88

Falklands War 34
Fanshawe, David 14
Fildes, Christopher 103
Financial Times, The 98
First World War 36-37, 48, 125
Fortier, Kimberley 103
France 37, 41-43, 54-55, 58, 62, 87, 88, 97-98, 117
Fraser, General Sir David 13-16
Freda Rebecca mine 77

Furness, Lord 69

Gass, David 81
Geita mine 81-83
George V 7
George, Eddie 6
George, Prince of Denmark 13
Germany 47-48, 53-54, 70 *see* also Second World War
Ghana 57, 63, 81, 85, 94
gold 47 *see also* Ashanti Goldfields, Baomahun mine, Freda Rebecca mine, Geita mine, Kalsaka mine, Mali Green mine, Peach Tree mine, Royal Family mine
Goldsmith, Major Frank 42
Goldsmith, Sir Jimmy 34, 39-40, 42-43
Goldsmith, Gill 42-43
Goldsmith, Teddy 34, 42
Goodison, Sir Nicholas 115, 116, 118

Villiers, Nicholas 15, 17, 21-22

Waddell-Dudley, John 3
Wallis, Michael 18
Watkinson, Terence 85
Waugh, Evelyn 21, 33, 54
Welby, Sir Anthony 66-68
Welby, Justin *see* Archbishop of Canterbury
Welensky, Sir Roy 59
Wellington Barracks 1, 13, 36, 73
Welsh Guards 31
Wernher, Beit & Co. 47-48
Wernher, Major General Sir Harold 48-49
Wernher, Sir Julius 47-48
Wernher, Lady Zia 48-49
Westminster, Duke of 19, 50
Whitbread, Loopy 34
White Cliffs Sparking Wine 125

White, Gordon 39-40
White, Sam 41-44
White's Club 37, 76
Who's Who 65
Williams, Charles 4
Williams, Jane 4-5
Wilson, Harold 4
Winston, Harry 86, 89
Winston Mines 89
Winston, Ronald 86, 89
Wodehouse, Ethel 53, 55
Wodehouse, P. G. xii, 53-56, 124
Wontner, Sir Hugh 17
Wontner, Jennifer 17
Wright, Stanley 31

Zanuck, Darryl 24
Zanzibar 82
Zanzibar Club 82
Zimbabwe 63-64, 75-81, 94 *see also* Rhodesia

Algy Cluff

Unsung
Heroes

... and a few villains

FOREWORD BY

Simon Heffer

From the Foreword by Simon Heffer

'What flows from these pages are not just good
stories about fine people, but a strong sense of
what the author has in common with them – a
sense of humanity and service. He also laments
the passing of types that adorned our lives but,
in a very different age, hardly now do so at all.'

Algy Cluff

Get On
With It

A Memoir

FOREWORD BY
A. N. Wilson

From the Foreword by A. N. Wilson

There's nothing worth the wear of winning,
But laughter and the love of friends

'Algy's life bears this out. This book is the opposite of a misery memoir. It rejoices in his kind
parents, his good friends and his happy marriage with three splendid sons. His boldness
in the field of business and his merriment as a
companion have their reward.'